SILENT DEATH

The **THREAT** of **CHEMICAL** and **BIOLOGICAL TERRORISM**

KATHLYN GAY

Twenty-First Century Books
Brookfield, Connecticut

Library of Congress Cataloging-in-Publication Data
Gay, Kathlyn.
Silent death : the threat of chemical and biological terrorism / Kathlyn
Gay.
p. cm.
Includes bibliographical references and index.
ISBN 0-7613-1401-6 (lib. bdg.)
1. Chemical warfare—Juvenile literature. 2. Biological warfare—Juve-
nile literature. 3. Terrorism—Juvenile literature. 4. Urban warfare—
Juvenile literature.[1. Chemical warfare. 2. Biological warfare. 3. Ter-
rorism.] I. Title.

UG447 .G34 2001
358'.34—dc21

00-041807

Published by Twenty-First Century Books
A Division of The Millbrook Press, Inc.
2 Old New Milford Road
Brookfield, Connecticut 06804
www.millbrookpress.com

CONTENTS

CHAPTER 1
The THREAT

You turn on the television and a news story is just breaking. Thousands of people in Chicago are being admitted to hospitals with symptoms that resemble those of pneumonia. Most patients have high fevers and can scarcely breathe. In nearly all the cases, patients attended a major concert at Soldier Field, but there appears to be no apparent cause for the epidemic. Some speculate the crowd of 60,000 was exposed to some type of "killer germs" released from aircraft while the concert was in progress. A much more detailed fictional event was presented by Thomas Inglesby, a physician at Johns Hopkins Center for Civilian Biodefense Studies. His imaginary tale begins on a November evening. The setting is a professional football stadium in the northeastern United States. An audience of 74,000 is watching a game.

> The evening sky is overcast, the temperature mild, a breeze blows from west to east.
> During the first quarter of the game, an unmarked truck drives along an elevated highway a mile upwind of the stadium. As it passes the stadium, the truck

releases an aerosol [spray] of powdered anthrax over 30 seconds, creating an invisible, odorless anthrax cloud more than a third of a mile in breadth. The wind blows the cloud across the stadium parking lots, into and around the stadium, and onward for miles over the neighboring business and residential districts. After the anthrax release, the truck continues driving and is more than 100 miles [160 kilometers] away from the city by the time the game is finished. The anthrax release is detected by no one.

Approximately 16,000 of the 74,000 fans are infected by the anthrax cloud; another 4,000 in the business and residential districts downwind of the stadium also are infected. After the game, the fans disperse to their homes in the greater northeast metropolitan area; some return to homes in neighboring states. . . . The driver of the truck and his associates leave the country by plane that night. They will be [far] away by the time the first symptoms of anthrax appear 2 days later.[1]

Before this story ends, anthrax has sickened thousands of those originally infected, and four thousand have died within ten days of the attack. The metropolitan area is in panic. City workers from firefighters to bus and subway operators are absent due to illness or death. Hospitals are crowded, and antibiotics to treat anthrax are in short supply.

Anthrax is a disease caused by the bacterium *Bacillus anthracis*, which forms a long-lived spore (sometimes surviving indefinitely) that can kill if inhaled unless antibiotics are administered immediately. There are several forms of anthrax, but the form that is inhaled (inhalation anthrax) is extremely deadly—"less than a thimbleful dispersed in the air could potentially kill hundreds of people," according to a Mayo Clinic microbiologist.[2] The anthrax, however, has to be specially dried and milled before it can be spread about effectively in an aerosol container, or sprayer.

Anthrax contamination is a common feature in many other likely acts of terrorism—that is, violence or the threat of violence against unarmed civilians or military troops to intimidate them. Terrorists use these acts or threats in attempts to accomplish their own political, religious, or other goals. "A terrorist who managed to break a flask of anthrax spores onto a subway track [for example] could quickly contaminate a large and conveniently confined volume of air . . . several thousand people could breathe in an infectious dose—far more than the number likely to be hurt or killed by a conventional bomb."[3]

Biological agents can cause not only anthrax, but also such diseases as plague, which is contagious, and botulism, or poisoning caused by bacteria in food. (A table of some biological weapons agents is at the back of this book.) Anthrax is one of the most insidious diseases, however. It affects sheep and cattle and sometimes humans who handle animals infected with *Bacillus anthracis*. As a weapon, anthrax spores in droplets of 1 to 5 microns (1,000 microns equals 1 millimeter, or .039 inch) dispersed in a mist can trigger a pneumonia-like disease in people. Those infected would suffer such symptoms as fever, vomiting, and a strangling cough. If patients receive antibiotics in the earlier stages of the disease, they are likely to be cured. But without antibiotics, infected people die within a few days from respiratory failure, hemorrhage (excessive bleeding), or toxic shock.

In recent years possible terrorist attacks with biological and chemical weapons have received much attention in the United States, and concerns about these threats are discussed in this book. Along with these concerns, this book includes some methods used to counter terrorist threats, such as the application of new technology, increased intelligence efforts, and the development of numerous domestic defense measures. A major factor in countering terrorism, however, is the ongoing international arms-control effort—preventing the spread of weapons of mass destruction.

WEAPONS OF MASS DESTRUCTION

During the Cold War, from the mid-1940s through the 1980s, with its intense rivalry between Communist and non-Communist countries, the threat of a possible nuclear bomb attack was ever present. But any nation or group planning to use the bomb also feared reprisal—and still does—which has helped prevent a nuclear holocaust, or massive destruction. However, nuclear bombs are still the most powerful weapons of mass destruction (WMD).

Bruce Hoffman, author of *Inside Terrorism* and director of the Washington office of the RAND Corporation, a research organization, contends that nuclear warheads are the only *real* WMD. But the U.S. government and most of the popular media include as WMD chemical and biological agents (such as anthrax) as well as radiological agents—lethal doses of radiation absorbed by the body within a short time period. According to Jessica Stern, a former member of the National Security Council staff:

> The U.S. government considered developing radiological weapons during World War II, but abandoned the project as impractical. Unlike chemical and biological agents, radioactive poisons act slowly. Depending on the source and concentration . . . the victim may feel no ill effects for months or even years. Moreover, radiological agents are difficult to disseminate in concentrations sufficient to cause death, radiation sickness, or cancer.[4]

Many law-enforcement and weapons experts believe that conventional explosives—bombs—are the most likely terrorist threat. In fact, most terrorist incidents in the United States have involved explosive devices, tear gas, and pipe and fire bombs. Government officials were clearly concerned about a terrorist bombing as the year 2000 approached. In December 1999 the U.S. Department of State announced that the government had credible information that terrorists were "planning attacks specifically targeting American citizens" through early January 2000. The department warned Americans traveling abroad to be alert, avoid large crowds, and vary their travel routes.

Adding to the U.S. government's concern was the arrest by Jordanian authorities of thirteen suspected Middle East terrorists who may have been part of a plan to bomb tourist sites and tour buses in Jordan. In addition, Algerian-born Ahmed Ressam, who was trying to smuggle explosives from Canada to the United States in December, and two other suspects were arrested by U.S. law-enforcement officials. According to a *Newsweek* report, federal authorities suspect that

> Ressam is part of an international plot, the outlines of which remain vague, but nonetheless ominous. They say he has ties to an Algerian extremist group, and the CIA [Central Intelligence Agency] believes that he may be linked as well to Osama bin Laden, the wealthy Saudi businessman indicted . . . in the 1998 bombing of American embassies in Kenya and Tanzania. Bin Laden, who is now living in Afghanistan . . . has declared a holy war and hopes to inspire Muslims to kill Americans everywhere.[5]

In spite of possible bomb threats, a number of polls show that most Americans are more concerned about attacks with biological and chemical (BC) agents. Some experts also fear that a major biological assault is near at hand and are surprised that one has not already occurred. Such an assumption stems partly from the fact that there is widespread knowledge regarding biological technology (biotech). Tens of thousands of technicians worldwide are able to develop biological agents based on the work that has been done in the laboratories of biotech industries and universities. As a result, countries with limited funds and only conventional military capabilities can produce BC weapons—often called a poor nation's "bombs"—fairly easily and inexpensively.

PRODUCING AND USING BIOLOGICAL AND CHEMICAL WEAPONS

Perhaps the most convincing reason to fear a major attack stems from actual incidents that demonstrate how organized terrorists and some national leaders seeking power or revenge produce, use, or plan to use these silent weapons. For example, during the devastating war between Iran and Iraq from 1980 to 1988, Iraqis used chemical weapons (CW) against Iranians. In the 1990–1991 Persian Gulf War, Iraq produced and planned to use not only CW but also biological weapons (BW). Strategic analyst Avigdor Haselkorn notes in his 1999 book that Iraq's chemical and biological weapons were designed to deter intervention when Iraq invaded Kuwait. Haselkorn argues that "the mere presence of such weapons in the region had a profound impact" on the outbreak, end, and aftermath of Operation Desert Storm, as the armed conflict was called. Even though a major goal of the Gulf War was to

> disarm a dangerous dictator of his mass destruction weapons, in its wake the proliferation [spread] of such weapons received a material boost. Today Iraq is still

believed to possess at least the components of chemical and biological weapons and long-range missiles. Worse yet, extremist regimes from North Korea in the east to Libya in the west are energetically developing similar or even more frightening munitions.[6]

In 1994 and 1995, Japanese citizens in Tokyo and other cities were terrorized by chemical attacks planned and executed by members of the Aum Shinrikyo (Supreme Truth) religious cult and its leader Shoko Asahara, who called himself "Holy Pope." The group hoped to spark a major war by attacking the Japanese Diet, or legislature, and other authorities as well as the U.S. Naval base at Yokosuka. In March 1995, cult members placed plastic bags of diluted sarin, a lethal gas, on crowded Tokyo subway trains during the morning rush hour. After the nerve agent was released, twelve people died and thousands were contaminated. Later, Japanese police discovered that the cult had stored tons of chemicals used to make sarin. In addition, they had secretly produced biological agents such as anthrax spores and a botulinum toxin. Technically the toxin from the bacterium *Clostridium botulinum* is not a biological agent, because it does not multiply but instead produces botulin, a poisonous substance. Cult members were attempting to develop a method to spray these agents over populated areas.

In 1994 rebels in the Russian republic of Chechnya began an insurrection, demanding their independence from Russia. After months of fighting, some of the rebels placed a canister of cesium—a radioactive material—in a Moscow flea market during the busy Christmas season of 1995. Apparently the intent was to expose passersby to radiation. However, someone alerted police, who located the container before anyone was harmed.

In August 1998, American cruise missiles struck the Shifa pharmaceutical plant in Sudan where, intelligence sources claimed, chemicals such as those used to produce extremely dangerous VX gas were being manufactured.[7] One drop of VX can be lethal. Missiles also struck the Zhawar Kili Al-Badr paramilitary training complex in Afghanistan. Described as "one of the most active terrorist bases in the world," the training camp is affiliated with Osama bin Laden. The American strike on these two sites was in retaliation for the bombings on August 7 of U.S. embassies in Kenya and Tanzania, which killed more than 260 people—among them 12 Americans—and injured thousands.

Whether organized terrorists or a rogue state—an outlaw nation—some group could find a way to produce and disperse biological and chemical weapons. Former U.S. Central Intelligence Agency (CIA) Director John Deutch explained to a U.S. congressional committee that "materials and knowledge to build chemical and biological weapons are today more than ever available. The possibility that a state [nation] or any other entity will use these weapons against the United States' interests is today more probable than in the past."[8]

U.S. President Bill Clinton often spoke of this threat. As he warned in a 1998 speech before the United Nations General Assembly:

> The new technologies of terror and their increasing availability, along with the increasing mobility of terrorists, raise chilling prospects of vulnerability to chemical, biological, and other kinds of attacks, bringing each of us into the category of possible victim. This is a threat to all humankind.[9]

CHAPTER 2
CHEMICAL WEAPONS and Their EFFECTS

ver since the Persian Gulf War of 1991, thousands of veterans of that conflict have suffered ailments that many blame on exposure to toxic chemical agents or to antidotes (prescribed drugs) taken to protect them from the release of CW. The Gulf War was prompted by an Iraqi attack on neighboring oil-rich Kuwait. To counter Iraq and defend Kuwait, the United States and a coalition of nations sent troops to the Middle East. Following a massive military buildup, Kuwait's independence was restored after only six weeks of air strikes and a few days of ground attacks.

The war's end, however, brought no relief to tens of thousands of veterans in the United States, Canada, and Europe. Since the veterans have returned home, they have complained of debilitating illnesses that include chronic fatigue, severe joint pain and headaches, intestinal problems, internal bleeding, and memory loss. These combined symptoms have been labeled the "Gulf War Syndrome," and U.S. military and Veterans Administration (VA) doctors told veterans that they were suffering from "stress" or psychological problems as the result of combat. Most veterans were advised to seek psychological counseling. Relatively few received treatment for their physical ailments or help from the Veterans Administration.

By 1993 ailing veterans and some of their family members, who also suffered unexplained illnesses, along with numerous supporters had begun to organize. They presented their cases to the news media and posted their stories on the Internet—and are still doing so. The Vietnam Veterans Home Page is listed along with other Internet Web sites at the back of this book.

Although the U. S. Department of Defense (DOD) and the VA repeatedly denied that veterans suffered from chemical poisoning, several members of Congress called for hearings on the subject, and an independent commission conducted a study of the Gulf War Syndrome. Eventually in 1995 the DOD admitted that thousands of Gulf War soldiers were exposed to chemical weapons, probably when Iraqi arsenals (some of which were known to contain CW) were destroyed by the U.S. military. Soldiers may also have been damaged by an experimental drug called pyridostigmine bromide, or PB for short. PB was taken to protect against attacks of nerve agents soman, tabun, and sarin. Military officials in the Persian Gulf were concerned that Iraq might use sarin, but PB is not effective against this potent gas. According to the office of U.S. Senator Jay Rockefeller, who cosponsored legislation to limit the use of PB:

> scientific studies have shown that PB, when combined with stress or other chemical agents—including the insecticide DEET, which U.S. troops applied to their uniforms and bodies—may be a factor in the variety of severe, debilitating illnesses facing many Gulf War veterans.[1]

No one has yet been able to show the exact cause of the Gulf War Syndrome, but a 1999 study of two small groups of sick Gulf War veterans suggests that exposure to toxic chemicals could be responsible for the veterans' health problems. The study, which was conducted at the University of Texas Southwestern Medical Center in Dallas, found that the veterans had significant loss of cells in the brain stem, which controls some of the body's reflexes. They also suffered cell loss in the basal ganglia, which connects the brain with other parts of the nervous system. Cell loss in the brain stem may cause problems with attention or balance, while cell loss in the basal ganglia can cause depression, difficulty with concentration, and pain problems, Professor James L. Fleckenstein, who led the study, reported to several news media in late 1999.

WHAT ARE CHEMICAL WEAPONS?

Just about any chemical or chemical compound can become a weapon—if someone uses it for that purpose. The 1997 international treaty known as the Chemical Weapons Convention (CWC) defines all chemicals as weapons unless they are "intended for purposes not prohibited under this Convention." The treaty also declares that CW include: "Munitions and devices, specifically designed to cause death or other harm" by dispersing toxic chemicals. Each State Party (one who signs the treaty) is required to destroy its stocks of chemical weapons and its production facilities, including riot control agents such as tear gas.

In the words of the treaty a toxic chemical is "any chemical which, through its chemical effect on living processes, may cause death, temporary loss of performance, or permanent injury to people and animals." Thousands of toxic substances exist, but only a small portion—between seventy and one hundred chemicals—have been developed for warfare.

No costly military-industrial base is needed to create CW. Producers of CW can use inexpensive and commercially available equipment, although developing delivery systems is more complex and manufacturing nerve agents can be a complicated matter. But "a graduate student in chemistry should have little difficulty synthesizing" the proper chemicals, writes Leonard Cole, who teaches science and public policy at Rutgers University.[2] Because chemical agents can be produced easily at low cost, they are weapons of choice for nations with limited funds or for terrorist groups.

The CWC categorizes various chemicals that have the potential to be agents of mass destruction. At the top of the list are those that have few if any peaceful uses and are prohibited by the treaty. Two other categories include toxins or their precursors (forerunners) that have both beneficial and destructive purposes. These are called dual-use chemicals, and they are legal for commercial use but could be illegally converted to weapons. Any chemical could move from one category to another depending on its application. For example, common industrial chemicals can be combined to produce mustard gas, a weapon used in World War I. Another example might be a highly toxic insecticide sprayed or dumped on an area to deliberately poison people rather than to destroy insect pests.

BLISTERING, CHOKING, AND BLOOD AGENTS

Some chemical agents used for weapons are vesicants, or blistering agents, such as sulfur mustard (known by the symbol H,HD) and lewisite (L). They burn and blister the skin, eyes, and respiratory tract. If inhaled in large amounts, a vesicant blisters the windpipe and lungs, causing death.

Between 1915 and 1918, during World War I, Germany introduced both chlorine gas and mustard gas as chemical weapons, and the Allied forces responded with similar gas attacks, the first major instance of CW being used in a large-scale war. An anonymous U.S. soldier who spent his time in the trenches as part of the British Expeditionary Force, experienced a gas attack, which he described:

> A crawling yellow cloud that pours in upon you, that gets you by the throat and shakes you as a huge mastiff might shake a kitten, leaves you burning in every nerve and vein of your body with pain unthinkable; your eyes starting from their sockets; your face turned yellow-green.[3]

Chemical agents used in World War I caused more than 100,000 deaths and hundreds of thousands of injuries. Although between 10 and 12 million people died in the war due to explosives, the use of chemical weapons so incensed the world community that a treaty was drawn up to ban CW. Nevertheless, since the "Great War," as it was first called, chemical agents have been developed and stockpiled for use as weapons. Confirmed cases include the use of CW "by Italy in Ethiopia (1935–1936); by Japan in China (1937–1945); by Egypt in Yemen (1963–1967); and by Iraq in Iran and Kurdistan (1983–1988)."[4]

Two other types of chemical agents that stem from World War I are phosgene (CG) and hydrogen cyanide (AC). Phosgene, if inhaled, irritates the respiratory tract, causing fluid to build up in the lungs and choke a victim. Hydrogen cyanide poisons the central nervous system.

Some CW are variants of tear gases, known by their code names CS and CN, which were used during the

Vietnam War. Their use created international controversy because this was considered a violation of an international treaty known as the Geneva Protocol (described in chapter 5).

NERVE AGENTS

Among the most chemically lethal agents are organophosphorus compounds, more commonly called nerve agents; they block the transmission of nerve impulses and paralyze the nervous system. Usually colorless and odorless, nerve agents are in liquid or gas form. They can be easily absorbed by the body if mists or droplets make direct contact with the skin or are inhaled. Depending on the concentration, nerve agents can kill an exposed victim within a few minutes to two hours.

In the early 1930s, a German chemist developed organophosphorus compounds for use as pesticides. But these compounds, which are nerve agents, also had military applications. One of the first nerve agents developed was tabun, known as GA in the United States, and the Germans produced 12,000 tons during World War II. In 1938, German chemists synthesized the compound sarin, or GB in U.S. terminology, and in 1944 developed soman, or GD. It is important to note, however, that none of these nerve agents were used as weapons.

During the 1950s, chemists in Europe and the United States developed nerve agents that lasted longer and were called "persistent" agents. These potent substances were designed as CW but were also marketed for a time as insecticides until they were banned because they were highly toxic to humans. One persistent agent with the long, technical name O-ethyl S-disopropylaminomethyl methylphosphonothiolate, is known simply as VX. It is considered more toxic than any other nerve gas.

NERVE AGENT POISONING

Nerve agents can poison rapidly when inhaled or absorbed through the skin. They block an enzyme called cholinesterase. The enzyme breaks down acetylcholine, a substance that helps nerves communicate and contracts and relaxes muscles. With too much acetylcholine, muscles cannot relax—they can only contract.

In 1995, Dr. Jerry J. Buccafusco, director of the Department of Veterans Affairs Medical Center Neuropharmacology Laboratory, began a study of the health effects of long-term exposure to low doses of nerve agents. Dr. Buccafusco's work may help explain the causes of some of the health problems suffered by Persian Gulf War veterans. As the doctor explained: "We don't know very well the status of the neurochemistry in someone who has been poisoned over a long period of time. . . . The whole cholinergic system is almost totally shut down. It's sort of like a spring that has been coiled, waiting to spring out again."[5]

According to a report from the Medical College of Georgia: "Dr. Buccafusco's work likely has implications beyond chemical warfare; for instance, farmers who work with insecticides are exposed to essentially the same chemical warfare agents." In fact, parathion and Diazinon are organophosphate pesticides that have caused deaths among farmworkers who apply the compounds. As Buccafusco explained: "If a farmer walks out in the field and happens to inhale a whole bunch of these insecticides, he can die. On the other hand, you can have another farmer who is walking through the leaves, brushes up and gets some on his skin and he may do this for a period of a month or more. He looks normal . . . [but] has been poisoned slowly."[6]

Because organophosphates often concentrate in the soil and can become hazards, Texas A&M University scientists have developed an enzyme that can diminish the poisonous effects of the pesticides. The U.S. Army helped fund the research, hoping that the enzyme could also be used to neutralize the effects of chemical weapons as well as clean up toxic residues in agriculture.

If you were ever exposed to a high dose of a nerve agent, you'd likely experience a variety of symptoms. You would have a runny nose, feel a tightness in your chest, and begin to drool. Your vision would become impaired and you'd have a headache. Your speech would slur. Sweating profusely, you'd feel queasy, get intestinal cramps, and vomit. You might also lose control of urination and defecation. In the final stages of poisoning you'd have tremors—jerk and twitch—and perhaps lapse into a coma. Finally, the poisoning process would affect the respiratory muscles and central nervous system, and you would suffocate and die.[7]

During the Iraq-Iran war of the 1980s, the effects of Iraq's deliberate CW attack on some of its own citizens were shown in TV broadcasts. Saddam Hussein ordered his troops to retaliate against the city of Halabja, whose primarily Kurdish population sympathized with Iran. Halabja was blitzed with a mixture of mustard gas and nerve agents sarin, tabun, and VX. An estimated five thousand people died immediately, and many of the survivors became extremely ill. But there was little follow-up on the long-term effects of that gas attack until the TV program 60 Minutes aired in early 1998.

The program helped prompt a British professor of medical genetics, Christine Gosden, to visit the town. "I was particularly concerned about the effects [of CW] on the women and children," Gosden wrote. "Most of the previous reported exposures to chemical weapons and mustard gas had involved [military] men . . . chemical weapons had never been used on this scale on a civilian population before. I was worried about possible effects on congenital malformations, fertility and cancers."

What Dr. Gosden found was "far worse" than she had imagined. Victims suffered from numerous ailments such as blindness, many types of cancers, miscarriages, birth defects, infant deaths, severe depression, neurological damage, and respiratory problems. Comparing the incidences of these health problems with those in a neighboring city, Dr. Gosden found the frequencies of most diseases three or four times higher in Halabja.[8]

DISPERSING CHEMICAL AGENTS

When used as weapons, chemical agents are usually dispensed from aircraft or from cruise missiles. But the extent of chemical dispersal depends on the method of distribution and such factors as weather, geographic conditions, and the number and types of buildings present.

The Organisation for the Prohibition of Chemical Weapons (OPCW) was set up to implement the CWC on an international level. OPCW describes the dispersal of chemical agents on its Internet Web site. When CW agents are released a mixture of liquid droplets and gas is generated. "The largest droplets fall and cause ground contamination whereas the very small droplets remain suspended as an aerosol. Together, the aerosol and gas form a primary cloud which drifts in the wind."[9] As would be expected, unprotected people close to the contaminated area would suffer injuries. If wind velocity is high, the cloud will pass fairly quickly, reducing dangers to people; low wind velocity, on the other hand, means the cloud hovers for a longer period and spreads its effects over a greater area.

Dangers from toxic clouds also increase when the terrain is soft, allowing contaminants to remain in the soil, or when the target area contains natural depressions or narrow streets. A dense stand of trees can help reduce the droplets or aerosols by "capturing" toxins in their crowns, or upper branches.

Weather determines how effective chemical agents will be. In winter, snow contaminated with chemical agents can collect on shoes and clothing and be taken inside buildings, tents, and vehicles. "Once in the warmth, the CW agent will evaporate and may cause dangerously high concentrations of gas." The danger of contamination diminishes with heavy rains, unstable air, variable wind direction, or temperatures below 32° Fahrenheit (0° Celsius). Dry weather, steady winds, and temperatures above 68° Fahrenheit (20° Celsius) are factors that increase the danger of a primary cloud.[10] The hot, dry weather in the Persian Gulf may have been a factor in contaminating ground forces during the Gulf War, some experts say.

CHAPTER 3
The Most Dangerous
WEAPONS:
BIOLOGICAL

As the controversy continues over Gulf War illnesses, so does the threat of Iraqi development and concealment of chemical agents and biological weapons (BW). After the end of the Gulf War, a United Nations Special Commission (UNSCOM) was charged with investigating whether Iraq was abiding by UN Security Council resolutions. The resolutions require Iraq to destroy its stockpiles of chemical and biological agents as well as munitions filled with these agents. Numerous times since 1991, Iraq has rebuffed UNSCOM teams and curtailed arms inspections, barring or delaying entrance of UN teams inside facilities. As one UNSCOM report to the United Nations Security Council notes: "From the first UNSCOM inspections in 1991 until 1995 Iraq denied it had a BW programme and has taken active steps to conceal it from the Special Commission. These steps included fraudulent statements, forged documents, misrepresentation of the roles of people and facilities, and other specific acts of deception." In mid-1995, Iraq admitted having a BW program, and since then has submitted several disclosure statements to UNSCOM. But all have been found inadequate, deceptive, or incomplete.[1]

In late October 1997, Iraq announced that American members of the UN inspection team would have to leave. After inspectors returned several weeks later, they found that at some sites equipment had been dismantled and documents and other evidence destroyed. Tensions have risen steadily ever since.

CONTINUED IRAQI CONFLICTS

In spite of Iraq's agreement in February 1998 to allow UNSCOM unrestricted access to suspected sites, just months later, in August 1998, Hussein barred surprise inspections of newly discovered facilities where ingredients for biological and chemical weapons might be hidden. One U.S. inspector, Scott Ritter, a former marine, left his post. He accused Iraq of hiding weapons capabilities in other countries and urged world leaders to take a tougher stand against Iraq. The most "shocking thing" Ritter found in his seven years with the UN team, was "the extent to which the regime in Iraq had undertaken to develop biological weapons."[2]

In November 1998, Iraq stopped even routine inspections of facilities. President Hussein demanded that international economic sanctions against his country be lifted as a condition for allowing continuation of UN inspections. The sanctions, which were put into effect a little more than a week after Iraq invaded Kuwait, prohibit the sale of products other than food, medicines, and health supplies to Iraq.

Several times the UN has eased the sanctions somewhat. Hussein's demands, however, were condemned by UN members, and in November the United States was within minutes of dropping bombs on Iraq because it did not comply with all UN resolutions.[3] The following month the chief UN inspector, Richard Butler of Australia, announced in exasperation that Iraq was continuing to thwart UN weapons inspections, and on December 16, President Clinton and British Prime Minister Tony Blair ordered air strikes (called Operation Desert Fox) against Iraq. The objective was, in Clinton's words, "to degrade Saddam's weapons of mass destruction program" and "his capacity to attack his neighbors." After four days the strikes were called off, and Iraq's capability to use WMD reportedly was diminished.

Less than two weeks later, however, Iraq appeared to be even more combative, halting all cooperation with the United Nations. In the days following the end of Desert Fox, Iraqi war planes were flown several times into "no fly" zones. One of the zones was established in 1991 in northern Iraq to protect Kurds often attacked by Hussein's fighters; a southern "no fly" zone was set up in 1992 to prevent assaults against Shiite Muslims who want to overthrow Saddam. British and American planes have routinely monitored the areas for Iraqi infractions.

Just days before the end of 1998, Iraqi surface-to-air missiles were fired at British and American fighter jets. U.S. jets fired back with laser-guided bombs that knocked out antiaircraft artillery. No doubt confrontations with Iraq will continue, and military and foreign-policy experts believe Iraq will attempt to build up its biological, chemical, and nuclear arsenals as well as ballistic missiles to deliver them.

In December 1999 the United Nations Monitoring, Verification and Inspection Commission (UNMOVIC) was established to replace the former UNSCOM. The new commission is required to operate a reinforced, ongoing monitoring and verification system, address unresolved disarmament issues, and identify additional sites in Iraq to be covered by the new monitoring system.

THE DEADLY AGENTS

The crisis with Iraq has prompted numerous questions about biological agents. What are they? What effect can they have? Why are they so dangerous? How serious is the threat of germ warfare—that is, the threat of biological weapons being used for mass destruction? Are biological agents new weapons?

Many biological agents are used for beneficial purposes, such as developing antibiotics and vaccines. But when biological agents are designed to destroy, they are far more potent than CW. Biological agents include living organisms that can survive a long time (sometimes indefinitely), multiply in their target hosts (humans, animals, and plants), and cause disease. They also include by-products of living organisms, such as toxins, which cannot reproduce themselves but generally can disable or kill a victim within minutes or hours.

Biological toxins (sometimes referred to as botox) are among the most poisonous substances known, and a small quantity can cause massive destruction. Toxins, or poisons, derived from living organisms or produced by chemical synthesis include ricin, which comes from the seeds of castor bean plants. Another example is botulinum secreted from *Clostridium botulinum* bacteria. This toxin is often associated with food poisoning, and the first symptoms—nausea and diarrhea—could occur within hours. Without an antitoxin, victims of botulism die of respiratory paralysis.

Biological agents also include viruses, such as those that cause smallpox, yellow fever, equine encephalitis, influenza, and Ebola, one of the most deadly known to science. A 1995 outbreak of the Ebola virus in Zaire in southern Africa was attributed to natural causes but alerted people worldwide to the possibility of a deliberate attack by such a virus, which has no known cure.

Other biologicals that can be used for deadly purposes are fungi that destroy crops and other vegetation and rickettsia, which are similar to bacteria. Rickettsia cause such diseases as Q-fever, Rocky Mountain spotted fever, and typhus.

HISTORY OF BIOLOGICAL WEAPONS

Various forms of germ warfare are centuries old, and in some cases nature itself has waged war—been responsible for diseases that devastated huge populations. In Western Europe during the fourteenth century, a bacteria caused what became known as the plague, which killed millions. More than 20 million people died between 1918 and 1919 during an influenza epidemic that spread around the world. Since 1981 the HIV virus that causes AIDS has infected more than 29 million people worldwide, killing about 1.5 million each year.[4]

While numerous epidemics are attributed to natural causes, germ warfare and attacks with biological agents are the deliberate and hostile use of disease-causing organisms. One wartime practice in ancient times, for example, was infecting the enemy by tossing diseased bodies over the walls of besieged cities or into their water supplies. Another practice was smearing arrowheads with fecal matter to infect victims or launching clay pots filled with poisonous snakes onto ships. An oft-repeated example reportedly occurred in colonial America during the French and Indian Wars of the 1700s when the British gave enemy tribes (who were fighting for the French) blankets infected with highly contagious smallpox. The smallpox killed many Native Americans.

In more recent history, during World War II, the Japanese Imperial Army conducted brutal experiments with biological agents, which they used against China. The Imperial Army dropped plague-infected bombs on Chinese cities, creating outbreaks of the deadly disease. In other atrocities—particularly those committed by the infamous Imperial Army Unit 731—Chinese, American, and other prisoners of war were infected with diseases such as plague. Some of the Chinese prisoners were dissected alive, without anesthetic, so that Japanese examiners could determine the effects of the disease on body organs. Tens of thousands died because of these gruesome experiments. But the stories about the horrific research have been revealed only in recent years and are still not well known by the general public.

To determine what specific biological agents could be effective as defense weapons, the United States and Great Britain conducted research on BW and carried out a number of tests during World War II. British scientists developed the "capability to kill German cattle by delivering linseed meal cakes laced with anthrax through the flare chutes of aircraft. Approximately 5 million anthrax-spiked cattle cakes . . . were stockpiled."[5]

Between 1942 and 1943, the British conducted BW experiments on Gruinard Island, 3 miles (5 kilometers) from their anthrax research facility called "X-Base" on Gruinard Bay in Scotland. A secret government report, declassified in July 1999, shows that the British scientists were deeply concerned about their research facility. Because of the wartime shortage of trained employees, unskilled teenagers and adults worked at the base, and scientists feared that they were "playing with fire," endangering not only factory workers but also people in the surrounding countryside. After test bomb explosions on Gruinard Island in July and September 1942, the research hazards became apparent. An "infected sheep's carcass washed ashore from the island, [which] led to the deaths of seven cattle, two horses, three cats and up to 50 sheep in a nearby village."[6] The bomb tests were stopped, and Great Britain's BW program was discontinued in the late 1950s.

In the United States, experiments with biological agents included BW that could kill crops. Although no BW were used in Europe during World War II, joint British and U.S. programs were broadened to include development of offensive biological agents that could be used against humans. The United States ended its BW offensive program in 1969.

Nevertheless, a Biological Defense Research Program (BDRP) at Fort Detrick, Maryland, continues as part of the U.S. domestic preparedness program. Over the years numerous critics—from congressional committees to independent analysts—have expressed concern over the safety of workers at the army site as well as the environment where tests have been conducted. Concerns stem from press reports about previous BW tests between 1949 and 1969. The U.S. Army claimed: "The tests were intended to see how bacteria might spread and survive in a biological warfare attack. Contending that the tests posed no risks, the U.S. Army said that the bacteria and chemicals were harmless 'simulants' [imitations] of more lethal bioweapons," writes Leonard A. Cole of Rutgers University in his highly critical book *The Eleventh Plague.*

Cole points to more than two hundred open-air tests over major U.S. cities, including San Francisco, Minneapolis, and St. Louis. "Some tests were more focused, including the release of bacteria into the New York City subway system, into the Washington, D.C., National Airport terminal, and onto the Pennsylvania Turnpike." In spite of the army's claim that there was no risk, the so-called simulants were "known at the time of spraying to be capable of causing illness or death."[7]

THE THREAT OF
BIOLOGICAL WEAPONS

Although biological agents have been developed and sometimes put to deadly use throughout history, BW have not yet been employed on a massive scale. "Small incidents involving some ingredient of a potential weapon of mass destruction are fundamentally different from mass-destruction attacks," write the authors of *America's Achilles' Heel*, a study on international security. They point out that "biological and chemical agents are not weapons of mass destruction unless they can be effectively delivered."[8] However, the threat of BW is ever present today, because modern technology provides relatively easy means for producing and dispersing biological agents. Two security experts, Richard Danzig, who became secretary of the navy in November 1998, and Pamela Berkowsky of DOD write that

> much of the technology required to produce and "weaponize" [biological agents] is available for civilian or military use . . . . advanced systems are not required for the delivery of biological weapons . . . . low-technology methods, including agricultural crop dusters, backpack sprayers, and even purse-size perfume atomizers will suffice.[9]

The possibility of an attack with BW is terrifying to most people. Unlike explosives or chemical releases, an attack involving disease agents would probably not be recognized at first. Because disease-causing organisms have incubation periods of several hours to six weeks before symptoms appear, an attack of biological agents can be confused with a natural outbreak of a contagious disease. Another problem is that victims would not be located in one place. As the U.S. Department of Health and Human Services explains:

A strong public health network would be needed to piece together early reports and determine quickly what had happened. And once detected, the situation could overwhelm traditional local health systems, faced not only with the tasks of caring for mass casualties but also with the demands of even larger numbers of the "worried well" for treatment or vaccination.[10]

BW can also prevent troops from mobilizing because of illnesses and can create mass panic among civilian populations. If people are unaware that a BW attack has taken place, they have little opportunity to protect themselves. Even if targeted populations, such as a military unit, are able to defend against BW, they may be hindered by cumbersome protective clothing or the debilitating effects of vaccines or antidotes they have taken.

If ever a biological attack became a reality, spray devices would probably be used because they can spread clouds or vapors of tiny particles over a broad area. The World Health Organization once estimated that 110 pounds (50 kilograms) of anthrax spores in aerosol form could be dispensed upwind of an urban center of 500,000 unprotected people and in ideal weather conditions could potentially kill or disable up to half the population. Still there are drawbacks. Survival and the effectiveness of some bacteria depend on such factors as how cultures are prepared and preserved and whether atmospheric and weather conditions dilute or kill off agents.

ECONOMIC THREATS FROM BIOLOGICAL WEAPONS

Biological weapons may also be used to attack domestic animals (cows, hogs, sheep, for example), crops, or ecosystems. Such an attack would wage a "potentially subtle yet devastating form of warfare, one which would impact the political, social, and economic sectors of a society and potentially of national survival itself," writes Air Force Lieutenant Colonel Robert P. Kadlec, M.D., in *Battlefield of the Future.*[11]

Although there are many ways of controlling pests, an enemy nation could breed so-called superpests that are resistant to known pesticides and arrange to have them released in the United States. These pests could be designed to attack farm crops, pastureland, food animals, forests, and so forth. Food and forest industries in the United States provide income in the hundreds of billions of dollars each year, and if there is widespread crop or forest damage, economic losses could be great. Suppose, for example, a terrorist or other adversary targets a cash crop like cotton with such pests as the pink bollworm caterpillar. Forests that provide lumber might be destroyed by imported beetles. Not only would there be losses of valuable commodities, but many industries dependent on these goods would be negatively affected.

Food shortages could also result if, for instance, BW are used to attack cereal grains across the Midwest grain belt. Whiteflies could be released over southern California to devastate fruit trees by sucking juices from leaves, sometimes stripping a tree. Although there are pest controls available to fight the whitefly, large numbers of the insects might threaten to destroy the entire fruit crop in the area.

Farm animals could be attacked with BW causing shortages in meat and dairy products. In 1992 an unintentional infection of cattle demonstrated what could happen if there was a deliberate use of BW. Cattle from Central America were brought into the United States and later found to be infected with screwworm, which destroys the animal's hide and kills calves. Other cattle along the Mexico-Texas border soon became infected, causing ranchers to lose large sums of money.

While most developed nations are able to moderate or overcome the effects of BW attacks on food and other commodities, the economic impact could create political and social upheavals. In less developed countries the impact would be worse. As Kadlec writes: "History has recorded the chaos and instability created by such natural catastrophes as famines and epidemics." If BW were used for that purpose it would be the same as "waging low-intensity warfare."[12]

WHO HAS BIOLOGICAL WEAPONS TODAY?

Periodically since the 1980s the U.S. Department of Defense has prepared reports for Congress on the proliferation, or spread, of WMD, and how the United States should respond to the threat of these weapons. In May 1997, DOD issued "The Regional Proliferation Challenge" (available on the Internet), which details nuclear, biological, and chemical weapons (NBC) programs in various regions of the world as well as capabilities of nations to use these NBC. According to the Defense Department, BW programs have been established in perhaps a dozen nations, although an exact count is uncertain. Others—Canada, France, Great Britain, Japan, South Africa, and the United States—have renounced their programs.

Iraq is one of the prime suspect states with stockpiles of BW or the capability to produce them and had the most advanced BW program of any in the Middle East prior to the Gulf War. Other states in the Middle East and in North Africa have the highest concentration of emerging nuclear, biological, and chemical weapons and missile programs of any region in the world. Among these nations are Egypt, Iran, Israel, Libya and Syria. China, North Korea, Taiwan, and Russia also are suspected of continuing their BW programs.

The Soviet Union's BW program was supposed to be curtailed in 1972 when biological weapons were banned with the international Biological and Toxin Weapons Convention, often called the Biological Weapons Convention (BWC). Although the Soviets were among the early signatories of the BWC, they continued through the 1980s to maintain a massive BW development program, employing 60,000 people—many of them scientists and technicians—at its peak. During the late 1980s, the Soviets were researching the Marburg virus, which attacks "every organ and tissue in the body." In addition, the Soviets were developing compounds known as "bioregulators," which "could control human moods, heart rhythms and sleep patterns and that could be used to destroy an enemy army," according to a report in *The New York Times*.[13]

The Soviet research was part of a weapons program that included many laboratories, production facilities, and test sites. One of these was a six-story factory in now-independent Kazakhstan, which has halted its BW program. The huge Kazakhstan plant (now closed) is "on a desolate, wind-blown steppe of Central Asia" where enough anthrax bacteria were being produced to "kill every man, woman and child in America many times over." Next to the plant was the machinery used to fill and seal bomb payloads, proof, U.S. officials say, that BW weapons were being produced.[14]

American, British, and other officials had long suspected that the Soviet Union's BW program was continuing, especially after a 1979 outbreak of anthrax in the city of Sverdlovsk. Dozens of people died. For more than a decade afterward, the Soviets claimed the deaths were the result of tainted meat. But in the early 1990s, after the Soviet Union collapsed, Russian officials admitted they had violated the BWC and that there had been an accidental release of bacteria causing anthrax.

Russians who once worked on BW research and were able to secretly flee to the United Kingdom and the United States have confirmed that the Soviets violated the BWC. One defector, Dr. Kanatjan Alibekov (now known as Ken Alibek), was first deputy chief of Biopreparat, the Soviet state pharmaceutical agency. Since coming to the United States with his family in 1992, Alibek has provided the U.S. military and the CIA with information on biological weapons and has testified at congressional hearings. He has also detailed much about the Russian BW program in his book *Biohazard* published in 1999. Alibek writes that the primary function of Biopreparat

> was to develop and produce weapons made from the most dangerous viruses, toxins, and bacteria known to man. Biopreparat was the hub of a clandestine [secret] empire of research, testing, and manufacturing facilities spread out over more than forty sites in Russia and Kazakhstan. Nearly every important government institution played a role in the Soviet biological weapons program . . . . through our covert [hidden] program, we stockpiled hundreds of tons of anthrax and dozens of tons of plague and smallpox near Moscow and other Russian cities for use against the United States and its Western allies.[15]

Alibek has been called a betrayer by some fellow researchers in Russia, but in Alibek's view Russia "has betrayed its people" by making banned weapons and training physicians and teachers to kill. At the end of his book, he acknowledges, "I cannot unmake the weapons I manufactured or undo the research I authorized . . . .but every day I do what I can to mitigate [lessen] their effects."[16]

After the collapse of the Soviet Union, and intense pressure from the United States and Great Britain, the Russians began dismantling their offensive BW program. Russia also claims that stockpiles of BW have been destroyed.

ASSESSING THE THREAT

There is little doubt that biological agents can be significant weapons, whether they are used against people, livestock, or crops. Human pathogens—bacteria and viruses that cause disease—are fundamentally different from WMD such as chemical and nuclear weapons. As international security expert John Steinbruner writes in *Foreign Policy*:

> Pathogens are alive, weapons are not. Nuclear and chemical weapons do not reproduce themselves and do not independently engage in adaptive behavior; pathogens do both of these things.
>
> That deceptively simple observation has immense implications. The use of a manufactured weapon is a singular event. Most of the damage occurs immediately. The aftereffects, whatever they may be, decay rapidly over time and distance in a reasonably predictable manner. . . . The use of a pathogen, by contrast, is an extended process whose scope and timing cannot be precisely controlled. . . . A lethal pathogen that could efficiently spread from one victim to another would be capable of initiating an intensifying cascade of disease that might ultimately threaten the entire world population.[17]

Graham Pearson, former head of Britain's Chemical and Biological Defence Establishment, notes that military and civilian leaders the world over regard biological weapons with a great deal of uneasiness. Pearson quoted U.S. General Colin Powell when he appeared before the U.S. House Committee on Armed Services in 1993. Powell testified that the weapons system that "scares me to death, perhaps even more so than tactical nuclear weapons, and the one we have less capability against is biological weapons."[18]

Bill Patrick, who worked for nearly fifty years at Fort Detrick's germ warfare program but now alerts the public about biological terrorism, also declares that BW "scare the hell" out of him. Patrick is coauthor of an antiterrorism guide for emergency personnel titled *Jane's Chem-Bio Handbook* published by the Jane's Information Group in 1998. (The group was named for Fred T. Jane who began publishing British reference books a century ago.) In an interview with *The New York Times*, Patrick stated that he is certain BW will be used by a terrorist group or a hostile nation: "It's not if. It's when," he said. Still, when assessing the possibility, Patrick insists that more—much more—can be done in the United States to prevent the sale of biological agents and equipment for developing BW.[19]

That is also the view of a group known as Business Executives for National Security (BENS) who issued a special report, *Assessing the Biological Weapons Threat*, in February 1997. In an update at the end of that year, BENS concluded that some progress had been made to create better defenses against dangerous microorganisms, such as the development of new vaccines, but they contend no "coherent program" is in place. BENS calls for a stronger Biological Weapons Convention, "more robust programs" to detect BW and defend civilians against BW attacks by terrorists.[20]

Navy Secretary Richard Danzig agrees. In a *New York Times* editorial in mid-November 1998, Secretary Danzig emphasizes that the United States is "under-protected against weapons that don't explode," which he categorizes with the acronym NEW—nonexplosive weapons. Not only does he cite BW but also so-called computer viruses. Like their biological counterparts, computer viruses can "infect" a computer with commands to destroy files or an entire system, which can be catastrophic. He writes:

> These NEW weapons can often be countered or circumvented on the battlefield. But if used against civilians they can cause widespread disruption, panic and (in the case of biological weaponry) deaths that could be counted in the hundreds of thousands. While military forces have protective clothing, encrypted [coded] systems and other barriers to biological and information attack, civilians are almost nakedly exposed.[21]

On the other hand, some experts like Jessica Stern, a Fellow at the Council of Foreign Relations, contend that incidents of bioterrorism are likely to be rare. "This is especially the case for attacks intended to create mass casualties, which require a level of technologic sophistication" that few domestic groups possess. Stern notes that groups sponsored by nations "are most likely to be capable of massive biological weapons attacks," but the nation

> would presumably have to weigh the risk for retaliation. . . . governments cannot ignore this danger, the potential damage is unacceptably high. Because the magnitude of the threat is so difficult to calculate, however, it makes sense to focus on dual-use remedies: pursuing medical countermeasures that will improve public health in general, regardless of whether major biological attacks ever occur. This would include strengthening the international system of monitoring disease outbreaks in humans, animals, and plants and developing better pharmaceutical [medical] drugs."[22]

CHAPTER 4
International
TERRORISM

Terrorism is not a recently invented activity or even a recent term. It stems from the French Revolution in the 1700s and the reign of terror that prevailed to control those who opposed the revolution and the new government that was established. Over the decades, terror has been the means that many dictators have used to hold on to power and to get rid of dissidents—those who disagree with their political views.

Since the end of World War II, most nations in the world have experienced some type of terrorism. Yet identifying terrorists is not a simple matter, and in some cases terrorist activity may not be seen as such by those who are sympathetic to a particular cause. For example, some religious groups condone terrorist acts because they are convinced they are waging a "holy war" or carrying out a divine mission; violence, they argue, is justified against those who do not share their beliefs. Organized white supremacists and neo-Nazis (who admire the World War II German dictator Adolf Hitler) want a nation for whites only and commit terrorist acts against people of color, Jews, and others they consider "evil" or "outsiders." Some animal-rights activists believe terrorism is a way to protect and save animals from scientific experiments conducted in laboratories around the world; terrorism is also a way to call attention to their cause.

Most terrorist incidents worldwide involve bombs, grenades, guns, knives, and other "ordinary" weapons, but some assaults (such as the release of sarin gas in Tokyo) have clearly indicated that terrorists—whether sponsored by nations or acting on extremist religious or cultlike beliefs—could launch biological, chemical, or nuclear weapons against their perceived enemies.

In countries like Israel, Great Britain, and the United States, countering terrorism has become a serious security issue. Terrorism is now seen as a *"strategic threat to the internal stability—and even survival—of countries . . . a threat to the security of the whole international community, including the United States, the only remaining super-power in the global arena,"* writes Ely Karmon.[1] Karmon is one of the experts at the International Policy Institute for Counter-Terrorism (ICT), an academic center established in 1996 in Herzliya, Israel. ICT focuses solely on the issue of global terrorism and countering international terrorist attacks—those involving people or the territory of more than one country.

TERRORIST ATTACKS

The Anti-Defamation League (ADL) in its online "Terrorism Update" lists and describes numerous acts of international terrorism. Other Web sites, such as the Political Terrorism Database, the Federation of American Scientists' Intelligence Resource Program, and the U.S. State Department Office of the Coordinator for Counterterrorism (OCCT), also describe violent acts committed by international terrorists.

In April 1999 the OCCT issued its annual report on "Patterns of Global Terrorism," which includes a chronology of significant terrorist incidents worldwide. According to the report, most terrorist incidents were bombings. "There were 273 international terrorist attacks during 1998, a drop from the 304 attacks recorded the previous year and the lowest annual total since 1971. The total number of persons killed or wounded in terrorist attacks, however, was the highest on record: 741 persons died, and 5,952 persons suffered injuries." Most of the casualties were due to the bombings of U.S. embassies in Kenya and Tanzania.

The State Department noted that the United States has developed a counterterrorism policy that "was advanced aggressively during 1998." That policy outlined in the report is:

First, make no concessions to terrorists and strike no deals.

Second, bring terrorists to justice for their crimes.

Third, isolate and apply pressure on states that sponsor terrorism to force them to change their behavior. The Secretary of State has designated seven countries as state sponsors of terrorism: Cuba, Iran, Iraq, Libya, North Korea, Sudan, and Syria. In addition, the U.S. Government certified an eighth country—Afghanistan— as not fully cooperating with U.S. antiterrorism efforts.

Fourth, bolster the counterterrorism capabilities of those countries that work with the United States and require assistance.

This last element is especially important in light of the evolving threat from transnational terrorist groups. These loosely affiliated organizations operate more independently of state sponsors, although those relationships still exist. They are highly mobile and operate globally, raising large amounts of money, training in various countries, and possessing sophisticated technology. The United States must continue to work together with like-minded nations to close down these terrorist networks wherever they are found and make it more difficult for them to operate any place in the world.[2]

TERRORIST NETWORKS

A prime example of a terrorist network is the International Islamic Front for Jihad against America and Israel. The terrorist organization is supported by Osama bin Laden (or Usama bin Ladin), who has made no secret of his hatred for the two countries and wants to rid his homeland—Saudi Arabia—of the influences of the United States and its allies. Bin Laden has not only been linked with the bombings of the U.S. embassies in Africa but also such terrorist acts as

> the killings of Western tourists by militant Islamic groups in Egypt, bombings in France by Islamic extremist Algerians, the maintenance of a safe-house in Pakistan for Ramzi Ahmed Yousef, the convicted mastermind of the 1993 World Trade Center bombing, and sheltering Sheikh Omar Abd Al-Rahman (the Blind Sheikh), who was also convicted in the World Trade Center bombing. He has also been linked to the 1992 bombings of a hotel in Yemen, which killed two Australians, but was supposedly targeted against American soldiers stationed there; the 1995 detonation of a car bomb in Riyadh, Saudi Arabia, the 1995 truck bomb in Dhahran, Saudi Arabia, that killed 19 U.S. servicemen; and the 1995 assassination attempt on Egyptian President Hosni Mubarak.[3]

Unfortunately, until the United States retaliated with the August 1998 missile strikes against one of bin Laden's training camps in Afghanistan, few Americans—including news commentators—had focused on a mass attack by terrorist groups. Indeed, many critics of the missile strikes called them a tactic to divert public attention from President Clinton's personal difficulties and impeachment. Opponents also condemned what State Department officials called the new "war on terrorism." Such a "war" does not, critics say, include attacks against terrorists who, for example, are Israelis or Serbians. An editorial in *The Nation* argued that the "missile attacks on Afghanistan and Sudan are illegal and immoral—violations of international law and the UN charter. They reinforce the notion that Washington considers itself Cop of the World, a rogue superpower appropriating the right to bomb anyone at will."[4]

British reporter Robert Fisk, who interviewed Osama bin Laden several times between 1993 and 1997, points out that the man President Clinton labeled "America's Public Enemy Number One" was once called a "freedom fighter," especially when he

> brought his 9,000 Arab fighters to support the Afghans in their conflict against the Soviet occupation army, hacking out the mountain trails with his construction equipment, building hospitals and arms dumps. . . . Some of his current Afghan fellow fighters had been trained earlier by the CIA in the very camps that were the target of the recent US missiles—but whereas they had been called camps for "freedom fighters" when US agents set them up in the early eighties, now they had become camps for "terrorists."[5]

However, former Secretary of Defense Caspar Weinberger argues that the retaliation was "long overdue." In his view, if terrorist encampments are not targeted then leaders "such as Saddam Hussein and Osama bin Laden would be free to accumulate and use chemical, biological, nuclear and other weapons."[6]

Clark Staten, director of the Emergency Response & Research Institute in Chicago, and his staff have been reporting on transnational terrorism and stateless warfare since the late 1980s. Staten also backs the retaliatory measures, emphasizing that the United States is not against Islam, the religion. But he points out that

> Mr. bin Laden and his followers are certainly playing this "religion card" to his advantage. [And] there have been any number of terrorist acts carried out by violent splinter groups of Islamic fundamentalists, who publicly justify their actions by quoting selected excerpts from the Koran, and who issue illegitimate religious edicts called fatwas, that legitimize and encourage acts of violence against America and her allies.[7]

Steven Pomerantz, retired FBI chief of counterterrorism, states emphatically that propagandists "fronting for Middle Eastern terrorism" are at work trying to discredit the United States with charges of racism and bigotry against Muslims. "The truth is," Pomerantz writes,

> that the counter-terrorism policies and activities of the United States government are based on a careful review of the currently existing threat, combined with the history of terrorism directed against U.S. interests at home and abroad. The inescapable conclusion . . . is that, both historically and currently, the single greatest threat of international terrorism against the United States emanates from Middle East groups. This conclusion is based on fact—not bigotry.
>
> There is not a single person known to me who works in this field who believes that Muslims as a group are terrorists or work in support of terrorism. The overwhelming majority of the millions of law-abiding followers of Islam residing in the United States abhor terrorist violence with the same intensity as their fellow Americans of other religious faiths. To blame an entire population for the actions of an extremist fringe is both unreasonable and unconscionable.[8]

STATE-SPONSORED TERRORISM

According to the U.S. Department of State, the governments of at least seven nations sponsor or support terrorism in one way or another: Cuba, Iran, Iraq, Libya, North Korea, Sudan, and Syria. Some of these countries may not have provided arms or funds for terrorists in recent years, but they have allowed known terrorists to live safely within their borders. Other nations provide terrorists with funds, training, diplomatic facilities, and other support.

Boaz Ganor of the Institute for Counter-Terrorism (ICT) explains that during the last half of the twentieth century

> . . . terrorism has become a tool of states and even of superpowers. In some cases, states established "puppet" terrorist organizations, whose purpose was to act on behalf of the sponsoring state, to further the interests of the state, and to represent its positions in domestic or regional fronts. In other cases, states sponsored or supported existing organizations, thereby creating mutually profitable connections.[9]

COUNTERTERRORISM

In 1996 the U.S. Congress passed the Antiterrorism and Effective Death Penalty Act (AEDPA), which authorizes the secretary of state every two years to compile a list of foreign terrorist organizations. With such a designation an organization is not allowed to raise funds in the United States, and its members are barred from the United States. In October 1999, Secretary of State Madeline Albright designated twenty-eight groups as foreign terrorist organizations. These are:

Abu Nidal Organization (ANO)
Abu Sayyaf Group (ASG)
Armed Islamic Group (GIA)
Aum Shinriykyo
Basque Fatherland and Liberty (ETA)
HAMAS (Islamic Resistance Movement)
Harakat ul-Mujahidin (HUM)
Hizballah (Party of God)
Gama'a al-Islamiyya (Islamic Group, IG)
Japanese Red Army (JRA)
al-Jihad
Kach
Kahane Chai
Kurdistan Workers' Party (PKK)
Liberation Tigers of Tamil Elam (LTTE)
Mujahedin-e Khalq Organization (MEK, MKO, NCR,
     and many others)
National Liberation Army (ELN)
Palestine Islamic Jihad–Shaqaqi Faction (PIJ)
Palestine Liberation Front–Abu Abbas Faction (PLF)
Popular Front for the Liberation of Palestine (PFLP)
Popular Front for the Liberation of Palestine–General
     Command (PFLP-GC)
al-Qa'ida
Revolutionary Armed Forces of Colombia (FARC)
Revolutionary Organization 17 November (17 Novem-
     ber)
Revolutionary People's Liberation Army/Front
     (DHKP/C)
Revolutionary People's Struggle (ELA)
Shining Path (Sendero Luminoso, SL)
Tupac Amaru Revolutionary Movement (MRTA)[10]

The State Department also provides descriptions of
these organizations and their areas of operation, which
are included in Appendix B. In addition, the information
includes the number of members in the groups and any
aid received from external supporters.

Some groups have challenged the foreign terrorist designation as being unconstitutional. Opponents charge that the law prevents people from making donations to organizations that may provide humanitarian and educational services as well as take part in terrorist activities. In October 1998, however, the constitutionality of the law was upheld. As the ADL pointed out in its brief supporting the law:

> . . . there is simply no way to compartmentalize the supposedly "good" works of [terrorist groups] from the bad, and it is therefore entirely appropriate for the United States to bar the provision of material support to these foreign terrorist organizations, regardless of how one wishes or claims to believe that support will be used. Like guns, bombs, and rockets, money can be a lethal weapon. Terrorists depend on private donations, using them to purchase weapons and fund violent attacks against innocent persons throughout the world. Even when money is donated allegedly for "humanitarian" purposes, it remains a dangerous commodity . . . it serves to free up other money that can then be used to purchase weapons or in other ways to facilitate terrorism. Or, money that is donated, allegedly for humanitarian or educational programs, may well be diverted to directly support terrorist training and violent acts.[11]

Along with counterterrorism laws, the United States has hosted major international conferences on terrorism. Participants have discussed such problems as how to improve transportation security to prevent terrorist attacks and how to tag weapons so that chemical and biological agents can be detected (an international treaty requires that conventional explosives be marked with a detection agent). One such effort in mid-1999 was an international conference sponsored by the U.S. Department of State's Office of the Coordinator for Counterterrorism and the Council on Foreign Relations.

Held in Washington, D.C., the conference had three objectives: to promote international cooperation against terrorism; to share information on terrorist groups and countermeasures; and to discuss policy choices. Representatives from twenty-two nations in the Middle East, South Asia, central Asia, Europe, and Canada were invited to participate.

One of the topics discussed was the political, religious, and sociological roots of terrorism in South Asia and the Middle East. The threat from religious extremists was another discussion topic. Other topics included domestic and international counterterrorism efforts and antiterrorism programs in the United States and other countries.

Along with the United States, other countries are attempting to set up safeguards against terrorism by enacting antiterrorist legislation and jailing known terrorists. In 1998, for example, Israeli businessman Nachum Manbar was convicted of selling materials for chemical weapons to Iran and sentenced to sixteen years in prison. In Germany Karl-Heinz Schaab was arrested and charged with selling plans for constructing a uranium enrichment plant and other nuclear technology to Iraq. Egyptian, Turkish, French, and Albanian officials also have jailed members of various international terrorist organizations during 1998.[12]

International cooperation is another important element in countering terrorism. Most of the eleven major international treaties on terrorism require signatory nations to bring criminal charges against terrorists who, for example, hijack a plane, take hostages, kidnap or murder "an internationally protected person" such as a minister of foreign affairs or national representative. Other criminal offenses include aircraft and ship sabotage. The treaties also require "parties to assist each other in connection with criminal proceedings" that are brought under any of the conventions.[13]

Additional cooperative efforts between nations include reviews of treaties, such as the BWC. Reviews provide opportunities to strengthen commitments to ban weapons of mass destruction. Nations also can cooperate with each other by sharing information about terrorists and their fund-raising efforts with law enforcement agencies in allied countries.

Another cooperative effort is a program established in 1995 by the U.S. National Academy of Sciences (NAS). Funded by DOD, the program encourages joint research between Russian and American biologists. Because thousands of formerly well-paid and high-status scientists in Russia have been laid off or are now working at low pay, American officials have been worried that Russian scientists would be tempted to work for other nations' BW programs. To stem the so-called brain drain, the NAS pays Russian scientists a stipend of $300 to $500 per month for cooperative research with Americans on biological agents that can be used for peaceful purposes. Russians are able to stay in their own country and Americans have been able to learn more about defenses against biological weapons.[14]

In spite of all the international and national offensive and defensive measures, the U.S. DOD warns that terrorism

> is a struggle that ultimately is fought in the political arena and, as such, is also a war of ideas and ideologies. Combating terrorism requires patience, courage, imagination, and restraint. Perspective is essential. Overreaction and bombast play into terrorist hands. Good intelligence, a professional security force, and a measured response are necessary. Most important for any democracy in its struggle against terrorism is a public that is informed and engaged, and understands the nature of the threat, its potential cost, and why the fight against terrorism is its fight too.[15]

CHAPTER 5
DEFENSE
Measures

hen troops went to the Persian Gulf in 1991, they were not well prepared for chemical or biological warfare, and would no doubt have suffered massive losses if nerve gases and germ agents had been released by Iraq. A report to Congress in 1996 from the General Accounting Office found that military emphasis on BCW defenses continued to be "insufficient to resolve continuing problems." But since 1996, the U.S. military has stepped up its efforts to improve defenses against BCW.

One of those defenses is the mandatory anthrax vaccination of the 1.4 million troops on active duty and 1 million reservists. The vaccine was approved by the Food and Drug Administration in 1970 and since then has been used safely by veterinarians, laboratory workers, and livestock handlers. Yet anthrax is only one threat, and federal and independent laboratories are attempting to develop more than a dozen new vaccines to protect U.S. forces. In addition, multiple systems for detection of biological and chemical agents are in development, production, or already in use.

The Department of Defense has contracted with a number of companies to focus on numerous aspects of CW and BW. One firm is the Chemical and Biological Information Analysis Center operated by Battelle Memorial Institute. It is involved in projects to identify the physical properties of agents, determine medical effects and treatment, study environmental effects, develop warning devices, and prepare for domestic attacks.

Since the mid-1990s, the Defense Advanced Research Projects Agency (DARPA) in the Department of Defense has been working on innovative BW and CW defense projects. One DARPA project is attempting to develop a remote-controlled sensor that would identify a large number of different biological or chemical agents in a given area. In the *Journal of the American Medical Association*, Dr. Jane Stephenson describes it as "a 21st-century version of the caged canaries used by miners to signal the presence of hazardous gases." The sensor uses nerve cells grown on silicone chips that monitor the cells' responses to neurotoxins in the environment.

In other projects, researchers are trying to find new ways to help the body develop its own immunity. Researchers also are attempting to develop a way "to use red blood cells to sweep up pathogens in the bloodstream and ferry them to the liver" for destruction, Stephenson reports. Still other scientists are studying "novel materials to be applied to the skin and mucous membranes or swallowed in a 'milk shake' to prevent pathogens and toxins from attacking the body." Such materials could also be used to decontaminate an area or sanitize a hospital.[1]

Access to extensive reference materials on biological and chemical agents is another major defense measure. Such information is contained in many books, but one is a huge volume titled *Jane's U.S. Chemical-Biological Defense Guidebook* or the more concise pocket guide *Jane's Chem-Bio Handbook.* The latter is designed for military teams, police, and others responding to real or suspected bio-chem attacks.

The army's handbook *Medical Management of Biological Casualties* is in printed format and is on the Web site for the Medical NBC (Nuclear, Biological, Chemical) Defense Training and Education Network. Designed for medical personnel to carry in their uniform pocket, the concise manual covers more than a dozen bacterial or rickettsia agents, the symptoms of the diseases they cause, medical management of these diseases, and measures used to prevent further contamination.

DOMESTIC PREPAREDNESS

Because biological and chemical attacks may go beyond traditional battlefields and include terrorist attacks on civilians, the U.S. military and numerous federal agencies have intensified their efforts to protect nonmilitary populations. The urgency for domestic defenses increased in the United States after such terrorist incidents as the 1993 bombing of the World Trade Center in New York City; the Tokyo, Japan, subway attack in 1995; the 1995 bombing of the U.S. Alfred P. Murrah Federal Building in Oklahoma City; and the bombing of American embassies in Kenya and Tanzania in 1998.

The Emergency Response and Research Institute (ERRI) in Chicago has maintained for years that local fire, police, and emergency services are not prepared collectively for a biological or chemical attack. Clark Staten of ERRI emphasized in 1997 that a "major consideration is the need for an effective pre-planning process." No one can predict the exact site of a biological or chemical accident or attack, but plans can be made for such an emergency. As Staten explains:

Logically, as in any crisis, the local Police, Fire depart-
ments and EMS [emergency medical service] agencies
will be immediately responsible for an operation
involving a chemical/biological release and mass casualties. But, depending on the circumstances of the incident, it may also be necessary to rapidly involve other
state and federal agencies . . . [including] the nearest
field office of the Federal Bureau of Investigation (the
federally designated lead agency in a confirmed
domestic terrorist event), the Secret Service, the
Department of Alcohol, Tobacco, and Firearms, state
disaster agencies, military units and specialized medical personnel/units . . . excellent interagency cooperation and communication is a necessity.[2]

In late 1998, Secretary of the Navy Richard Danzig
underscored that necessity by writing: "It is not likely
that our response to a biological threat against, say, Denver would or should be limited to the Denver Police
Department, or even the Federal Bureau of Investigation
or the Federal Emergency Management Agency. . . .
Only through a new union of our public health, police
and military resources can we hope to deal with this
dangerous threat."[3]

"MODEL" RESPONSE

In 1996 a pipe bomb exploded during a concert at Cen-
tennial Olympic Park, a popular site for those attending
the Olympic Games in Atlanta, Georgia. The explosion
had nothing to do with a BW or CW attack, but the
response by multiple agencies has been held up as a
prototype for ongoing efforts to safeguard civilians from
the effects of biological and chemical terrorism. Minutes
after the explosion in the park, hundreds of local firefighters, police, and medical personnel were on the
scene. Within hours FBI agents were at the site collect-

ing soil samples from the crater made by the bomb, pieces of shrapnel, and fabric from the bag that held the bomb. The samples were then analyzed at a DOD mobile and self-sufficient laboratory called the Science and Technology (SciTech) Center set up at the Centers for Disease Control (CDC) in Atlanta. According to a report in *Chemical & Engineering News*:

> Sci-Tech Center brought together under one roof the best chemical and biological warfare agent analytical capability to be found within the federal government. The Army contributed its Army Materiel Command Treaty Laboratory for chemical warfare agent identification; the Navy provided its Biological Defense Research Program for biological warfare agent verification.
>
> Counterterrorism is not the principal function of either lab. The Army's lab is set up to verify compliance with the Chemical Weapons Convention. The Navy lab, part of the Naval Medical Research Institute, conducts biological research.[4]

Between fifty and seventy-five chemists and biologists were on call for work at SciTech, and after the park bombing, both army and navy specialists shared their expertise in analyzing materials for biological and chemical agents. No such agents were detected.[5] This quick response and the cooperation between civil and military personnel are what federal agencies hope to accomplish with a so-called first responders program.

"FIRST RESPONDERS"

As the term suggests, "first responders" are emergency personnel who would be on the scene immediately after a weapons of mass destruction onslaught if it occurs. The Defense Authorization Bill, known as the Nunn-

Lugar-Domenici II legislation for the senators who sponsored it, was passed in September 1996 and provides funds to support state and local training programs for effective responses to possible WMD attacks. Secretary of Defense William S. Cohen said the program "is specifically designed so that the people we train become trainers themselves. This approach will greatly magnify our efforts to produce a core of qualified first responders across the nation."[6]

The program is administered by the U.S. Army Soldier and Biological Chemical Command (SBCCOM) at the Aberdeen Proving Ground in Maryland. SBCCOM is the Department of Defense's main agency for teaching those who will train state and local personnel how to respond to BCW. Initially the training focused on two dozen cities, among them Denver, Colorado; Los Angeles and San Diego, California; Houston, Texas; Chicago, Illinois; New York City; and Washington, D.C. Eventually a total of 120 cities throughout the United States will be involved at a cost of at least $100 million.

The FBI is the lead agency for crisis management should there be a terrorist attack and is charged with investigating the incident and preparing the criminal case for prosecution. Managing the consequences of a terrorist incident is the responsibility of the Federal Emergency Management Agency (FEMA). The agency would coordinate federal support of state and local governments in their efforts to protect public health and safety, restore essential government services, and provide emergency relief to affected governments, businesses, and individuals.

In March 1998, Secretary Cohen announced an additional DOD support initiative—the military's first-ever rapid assessment teams called RAID (rapid assessment, identification, and detection). Explaining the program, he said:

These new RAID teams will quickly reach the scene of
an incident in order to help local first responders figure
out what kind of attack occurred, its extent, and the
steps needed to minimize and manage the consequences.

Getting prepared for such a potential attack is
extremely complicated, given the wide range of possible threats and the many players at the local, state and
federal levels.[7]

RAID teams are stationed in ten regions of the United
States where FEMA has headquarters. These are located
in New York City; Boston, Massachusetts; Philadelphia,
Pennsylvania; Atlanta, Georgia; Chicago, Illinois; Kansas
City, Missouri; Denton, Texas; Denver, Colorado; San
Francisco, California; and Seattle, Washington.

In the event of a domestic attack, a RAID team would
appraise the casualties and damage in its region. For
example, the Pennsylvania National Guard team would
reinforce local first responders in the region that includes
not only Pennsylvania, but also Washington, D.C.,
Delaware, Maryland, Virginia, and West Virginia. RAID
teams also will determine what kinds of BCW were used
and whether they should call in additional support such
as reconnaissance or decontamination units.

Although federal officials have touted the domestic
preparedness program, some local and state participants and independent experts have criticized the effort
as inefficient and inadequate, according to a *Washington Post* report. Critics testifying before a 1998 congressional committee "complained that overlapping initia-
tives by the Pentagon, FBI and other federal agencies
caused confusion at the local level about who in Washington was in charge and where to go for more federal
assistance."[8] However, coordinating federal efforts is
the goal of the Justice Department and the FBI and their
National Domestic Preparedness Office.

SIMULATED ATTACKS

Since training for first responders began, emergency personnel in a number of U.S. cities have been conducting simulated terrorist attacks. Response teams act out what they would do if there is a release of deadly agents, such as setting up decontamination centers to prevent the spread of biological agents from one person to another. They also practice transporting victims to hospitals and carrying away the dead.

Some resources that would be used if a BW or CW attack occurred include portable showers so victims could decontaminate themselves in a water and bleach solution or some other disinfectant. Detection equipment would also be necessary. In New York City, for example, emergency teams used a mini-lidar sensor that is "designed to detect exposed chemicals, whether fluid, gases or even explosive powders, from a safe distance," according to a CNN report. "By using an ultraviolet laser, the lidar sensor can determine if the substance is biological or chemical. If it's chemical, it can tell exactly what it is by analyzing its light waves, and a computer then produces a graph or fingerprint of the chemical contents."[9]

Suppose your city or town received a warning that a BW or CW attack was imminent. Assume that first-responder teams would be ready to take action, and hospitals would have a sufficient amount of antibiotics, vaccines, and antidotes to treat victims. But what could or would an individual do?

To be effective, a personal defense system would require not only advance warning, but also a reserve of survival gear, some of which could be expensive. You or a family member might seal openings around doors and windows with tape or go into a specially prepared room insulated with plastic and ventilated with a system that filters the air. Each person in the household might put on a protective suit made of a material that contains disinfectants and can destroy bacteria and viruses. Well-fitting gas masks with filters that would block one-micron-size particles of deadly substances would be part of the protective gear. Your household likely would have respirators, disinfectants, and antibiotics on hand ready to use.

MEDICAL HELP

If anyone is exposed to a biological agent, extended treatment with antibiotics might be necessary. However, it is no simple matter for medical practitioners to figure out how to respond to an attack because there has been so little experience dealing with real cases. Doctors in the United States are not familiar with many of the diseases that could be caused by biological agents and may not recognize symptoms. Consider this: In industrialized nations few physicians have seen a case of anthrax or the plague. Smallpox might not be identified immediately because the disease was wiped out, with the last reported case in 1977. But the Soviets "cultivated tons of smallpox," in a secret laboratory where former Russian Ken Alibek and his colleagues "experimented with the culture until [they] came up with a weapons-quality variant." And a number of other countries may have obtained the smallpox virus from Russia, some experts believe.[10]

An important factor in domestic preparedness for germ warfare is developing awareness within the health-care community that a communicable disease may be caused by a deliberate release of BW agents rather than by a natural outbreak. Some steps have been taken to alert medical practitioners to the possibility that bacteria and viruses may be deliberately released and to show how infectious disease is not just a public-health issue but a basic national security problem. With that goal in mind, medical and scientific journals and Internet sites have carried numerous articles and studies on the topic.

The July–August 1999 issue of *Emerging Infectious Diseases*, published by the National Center for Infectious Diseases, was devoted to bioterrorism. It includes articles on "The Emerging Threat of Bioterrorism," "Congressional Efforts to Address Bioterrorism," "Vaccines in Civilian Defense Against Bioterrorism," "The Prospect of Domestic Bioterrorism," and "Historical Trends Related to Bioterrorism." The magazine's contents are available on the Internet.

The topic of biological warfare was covered in a special issue of the *Journal of the American Medical Association* (August 6, 1997). The issue includes a primer on BW, articles on diagnosis and management of infectious diseases caused by BW, and new developments in defenses against bacteria and viruses.

New Scientist magazine focused on BW terrorism in its February 28, 1998, issue. Along with other defense strategies, the magazine reported that some international researchers are suggesting that hospitals be equipped with "the type of high-tech detectors being developed to identify airborne pathogens on the battlefield. With a detector at each bedside, doctors could pick out the volatile molecules released by damaged lung membranes at a very early stage of infection and instantly tell whether a patient was a victim of a biological attack."[11]

The *Weekly Web Review in Emergency Medicine* is an Internet site that provides medical practitioners with information on articles and studies relating to emergency medicine. One posting, for example, described anthrax as a potential biological weapon, explained the types of treatments that could be used, and included links to important reading on the topic.

PREEMPT Medical Counter-Terrorism, Inc., also maintains a Web site. Founded in 1997, this nonprofit organization trains emergency medical personnel in how to respond to BCW assaults.

Dozens of other Web sites include medical information about BCW along with safety measures that can be taken. One site is Air Chronicles, which has posted the book *Battlefield of the Future: 21st Century Warfare Issues*, with four chapters specifically focusing on biological warfare and defenses against BW. Others are the Bradford Project on Strengthening the Biological and Toxin Weapons Convention and Preventing Biological Warfare; the Centers for Disease Control and Prevention; the Federation of American Scientists; and the United States Army Soldier and Biological Chemical Command. The Internet addresses for these and other sites are listed at the back of this book.

Perhaps the most important message in the various publications cited is that surveillance is crucial. Numerous experts have emphasized the need for a comprehensive intelligence effort, stepping up collection of information on the capabilities of a suspect nation or terrorist group to produce, store, and dispense BCW. Former senator Sam Nunn, who until his retirement in 1996 was a major force in developing legislation to improve BW defense and awareness, noted that there is no simple way to determine whether BC agents are being used for peaceful or military purposes. "It is not something you see with a satellite. It all turns on intent. That's why it is such a hard intelligence problem."[12]

Along with surveillance, verifiable arms control is a primary defense measure, say countless individuals, groups, and agencies. Indeed, numerous efforts have been under way for years to stop the spread of WMD, although it is likely that arms control can only be achieved on a limited basis.

CHAPTER 6
International
ARMS CONTROL

The spread of WMD and their means of delivery "pose an unusual and extraordinary threat to the national security, foreign policy, and economy of the United States," President William J. Clinton wrote in a 1998 letter to the speaker of the House of Representatives and the president of the Senate. In his correspondence, President Clinton advised the Congress, as required by law, that he had extended and amended a previous emergency executive order to "more effectively respond to the worldwide threat" of BCW. Clinton also outlined past arms control efforts and cited the need for strong international treaties and systems to detect weapons of mass destruction.[1]

TREATIES AND AGREEMENTS

For hundreds of years nations have attempted to eliminate chemical weapons through international agreements. In 1675, for example, the French and Germans agreed to ban poison bullets in warfare. By the 1800s, chemical weapons could be produced on a large scale, and several international treaties prohibited their use. But during World War I, there were large-scale attacks with poison gases, and at the end of the war several efforts were made to bring about an international agreement banning biological and chemical weapons. It was not until 1925, however, that representatives of forty-four nations signed a treaty called the Protocol for the Prohibition of the Use of Asphyxiating, Poisonous or Other Gases, and Bacteriological (Biological) Methods of Warfare. Negotiated in Geneva, Switzerland, it became known as the Geneva Protocol and went into effect in 1928.

The protocol states that chemical and biological weapons are "justly condemned" by the civilized world, which helped establish the idea that the use of CW and BW was not morally acceptable. Nevertheless some countries continued to use chemical weapons.

Although the treaty banned the use of biological and chemical weapons, it did not prohibit their manufacture, possession, or testing. Some countries, including the United States and the Soviet Union, developed and stockpiled substantial amounts of CW and BW. The United States, which was one of the early signatories of the Geneva Protocol, did not ratify the agreement until 1975, partly because of the fear during the 1950s and 1960s that the Soviet Union would launch attacks with BCW. When the Soviet Union and some other nations, including France and the United Kingdom, ratified the protocol, they declared that they would not be bound by the treaty if their enemies, or their enemies' allies, used chemical weapons first.

Since the 1925 Geneva Protocol numerous arms control agreements have gone into effect. Among the main international treaties that followed were the 1968

Nuclear Non-Proliferation Treaty (NPT), the 1972 Biological Weapons Convention (BWC), and the 1993 Chemical Weapons Convention (CWC). These and other agreements provide what U.S. Secretary of State Madeline Albright called

> the diplomatic framework guiding our efforts to prevent the spread and limit the dangers of the world's deadliest weapons. In fulfilling this mission, diplomacy is an important, but not our only, tool. When we negotiate arms control and nonproliferation agreements, we hope others will act in good faith. But we never count on this. We insist, instead, on the most thorough possible verification measures. We exercise our treaty rights to the full. And we maintain the world's strongest, best-prepared and best-equipped armed forces.[2]

BIOLOGICAL AND CHEMICAL WEAPONS CONVENTIONS

After World War II, international negotiations on arms control during the 1950s and 1960s usually grouped together nuclear, chemical, and biological weapons, as well as conventional weapons in a single disarmament package. Progress on disarmament was hindered because of differences over whether all WMD should be linked rather than treated separately. The United States and Great Britain, for example, wanted a separate treaty for biological weapons, stressing that chemical weapons, unlike BW, had been used in warfare and many nations maintained CW to retaliate in kind if attacked with CW. The Soviet Union and its allies argued for a treaty covering both chemical and biological weapons, insisting that the chemical arms race would accelerate if not dealt with in the BW treaty.

When U.S. President Richard Nixon took office in 1969, he ordered a review of BCW programs and policies. President Nixon declared that the United States would confine its biological program to research on immunization and other defense measures. He also ordered the DOD to get rid of U.S. stocks of biological agents and weapons and in 1970 extended the ban to toxins—poisons produced by bacteria or chemical processes.

Nations around the world praised the U.S. action, and Canada, Great Britain, and Sweden promised not to produce any BW. But there was general agreement worldwide that an international treaty was needed. By 1972 the Convention on the Prohibition of the Development, Production and Stockpiling of Bacteriological (Biological) and Toxin Weapons and on Their Destruction, a treaty better known as the Biological Weapons Convention (BWC), was ready for signatures. After President Nixon signed for the United States, he submitted it to the U.S. Senate, which by law must ratify any treaty. The Senate held up ratification until the end of 1974, when both the BWC and the Geneva Protocol were unanimously approved. President Gerald Ford signed both treaties in January 1975, and the BWC became effective in March 1975. By the end of 1997, 158 nations had signed the agreement.

Since the ratification of the BWC, the treaty has been periodically reviewed, and many security experts have expressed concern about the difficulties of verifying whether countries are complying with the agreement. Facilities for research, development, and production of BW and CW can be easily hidden in buildings that appear quite ordinary or in underground complexes.

Efforts to strengthen the BWC have been ongoing, and there are plans for an enforcement agency called the Organization for the Prevention of Biological Warfare, which will investigate alleged violations. Verification methods include mandatory reports on BW provided by signatory nations and interviews with people in charge of facilities (such as laboratories) using biological agents. In addition, visual inspection of facilities should indicate whether equipment, such as large fermenters, freeze-dryers, and aerosol inhalation chambers, are present and being used for BW production. On-site inspections could also include taking samples of dust and testing air filters inside a building and sampling soil, plants, and water outside a facility.

However, on-site sampling is a highly controversial issue. As microbiologist Raymond Zilinskas, who participated in the UN inspections for BW in Iraq after the Gulf War, noted: "To be effective, some on-site measures are intrusive. . . . This has led to concerns over protecting national security and intellectual property rights in the countries or facilities subject to inspection."[3] Inspectors could gather significant information about a company's or facility's projects and plans, which are rightfully private property. Thus on-site inspectors might be required to sign agreements promising not to disclose private data.

CHEMICAL WEAPONS CONVENTION

From the 1970s until 1997, the United Nations negotiated for approval of the Chemical Weapons Convention (CWC). Formally known as the Convention on the Prohibition of the Production, Stockpiling and Use of Chemical Weapons and on Their Destruction, the treaty bans an entire class of WMD and was ratified by the required sixty-five nations in 1997. By the end of the century, 126 nations had ratified the international treaty, which prohibits "development, production, acquisition, stockpiling, retention, transfer and use of chemical weapons." Under Article I of the convention, each signatory nation agrees to destroy any chemical weapons it owns or any weapons "that are located in any place under its jurisdiction or control," and also "not to use riot control agents [tear gas] as a method of warfare." Stockpiles of CW must be destroyed by 2007.

The CWC could have a major impact and widely affect the private sector, according to the ACDA. Even though the United States does not manufacture CW, it has a stockpile of such weapons, and U.S. factories produce and process chemicals that can be used for dual purposes. For example, a solvent used in ballpoint pen ink can be easily converted into mustard gas. To ensure that chemicals are not used for other than peaceful purposes, the CWC mandates that commercial facilities report where their chemicals are produced, how they have been consumed, whether chemicals have been imported, exported, or stockpiled. Reporting forms and inspection procedures were developed with the help of industry representatives who had legitimate concerns about secret company information, such as a manufacturing process, that is legally protected. The U.S. Chemical Manufacturers Association supports the CWC and inspection procedures, claiming that vital commercial interests will not be harmed.[4]

Who will conduct inspections? The UN's Organisation for the Prohibition of Chemical Weapons (OPCW) is responsible for implementing the treaty. State parties, or nations that have signed the agreement, are required to submit to the OPCW completed questionnaires regarding military and commercial chemical facilities. OPCW specialists will inspect declared facilities for storing, producing, and destroying chemical weapons. Inspection teams for the military will be made up of such specialists as "CW/Conventional Munitions Specialists, Chemical Production Technologists, Analytical Chemists and Medical Specialists." Industry inspection teams "would consist of . . . Chemical Production Technologists, Industrial Chemists, Chemical Production Logisticians (Material Resources Planning Specialists) and Analytical Chemists," OPCW reports. The treaty also "allows each State Party to have an international inspection conducted at any facility or location in any other State Party without right of refusal, at short notice, in order to clarify and resolve questions of possible noncompliance."[5]

NUCLEAR BANS

One of the earliest efforts to ban weapons of mass destruction was the Nuclear Non-Proliferation Treaty (NPT), which went into effect in 1970. This multilateral agreement—a treaty between many countries—is a legal deterrent to the spread of nuclear weapons. Signatories to the treaty agreed that any nation with nuclear weapons would not "transfer to any recipient whatsoever nuclear weapons or other nuclear explosive devices" and nonnuclear countries would not accept, manufacture, or "otherwise acquire nuclear weapons."[6]

When it was first negotiated in the late 1960s, only five nations had nuclear weapons—China, France, Great Britain, the Soviet Union, and the United States. Today, countries that have abandoned their nuclear weapons programs include Argentina, Australia, Brazil, Canada, Germany, Sweden, Switzerland, and former Soviet Union states. A few countries that did not sign the treaty—India, Israel, and Pakistan—have not declared their nuclear arsenals but possess them. In addition,

Iran, Iraq, North Korea, Libya, and perhaps Egypt, Syria, and Algeria have tried to acquire nuclear weapons.[7]

At the 1995 conference of the parties to the NPT, the majority of the participants representing the 175 signatory nations supported an indefinite extension of the treaty with reviews every five years. According to the U.S. Arms Control and Disarmament Agency (ACDA), which merged with the U.S. State Department in 1999, "The United States is strongly committed to the NPT" and efforts to further strengthen the treaty.[8]

In addition to reinforcing the NPT are international efforts to ban the use of plutonium and uranium for the manufacture of nuclear weapons. Negotiations have been under way since 1993 for a treaty that would legally bind signatory nations to end production of fissile material (plutonium and uranium) for WMD. As President Clinton noted in a 1997 message to the United Nations Conference on Disarmament, "effectively cutting off the spigot for more nuclear weapons is a necessary step toward, and would greatly contribute to, the ultimate goal of nuclear disarmament."[9]

Another major international agreement to bring about nuclear arms reduction is the 1996 Comprehensive Nuclear Test-Ban Treaty (CNTBT), which was negotiated over a two-and-a-half-year period. At the end of 1999, 155 nations had signed the CNTBT. By signing the agreement, each nation promises "not to carry out any nuclear weapon test explosion or any other nuclear explosion, and to prohibit and prevent any such nuclear explosion at any place under its jurisdiction or control." A CNTBT organization was set up to verify whether nations are complying with the treaty, using such methods as satellite surveillance and on-site inspections of nuclear facilities.

Yet, in order for the treaty to enter into force, forty-four nations must ratify it. President Clinton was the first to sign the CNTBT, but the U.S. Senate must vote on ratification. The Senate, in a highly political action, rejected ratification of the CNTBT in October 1999, which shocked many Americans and U.S. allies and friends. This was the first time in eighty years that the United States had rejected a major treaty. However, some U.S. senators and federal officials vowed to continue efforts to get a test-ban treaty signed, and the U.S. government has promised to maintain its suspension of nuclear tests, which have not been undertaken since the early 1990s.

Other important nuclear bans are bilateral, or between two parties. The Strategic Arms Reduction Treaty (START), for example, was negotiated between the United States and the Union of Soviet Socialist Republics (USSR) over a nine-year period. U.S. President George Bush and USSR President Mikhail Gorbachev signed the document in Moscow on July 31, 1991. After the Soviet Union dissolved, four independent states—Belarus, Kazakstan, Russia, and Ukraine—which had nuclear weapons facilities within their borders, became part of the START agreement. They also agreed to the Nuclear Non-Proliferation Treaty (NPT).

A START II agreement reduced nuclear arsenals even further, but it has not yet been ratified by the Russian Duma (legislature). Following ratification, serious negotiations will begin on a START III agreement to further control nuclear arms.

OTHER AGREEMENTS

Several other agreements between nations are designed to control exports of WMD and their means of delivery. One is an informal group of twenty-nine nations that have voluntarily formed the Missile Technology Control Regime (MTCR). Originally designed to control the export of missiles carrying nuclear warheads, the MTCR now tries to prevent the spread of missiles with BW and CW. Although member states have agreed to guidelines for denying transfer of various missile materials and technology, the guidelines are not legally binding. But national laws (such as the U.S. Arms Export Control Act) do include restrictions on the export of missiles and missile-related materials that would be used for delivering WMD.

The Australia Group is the name of another informal and voluntary consortium of nations; it was founded in 1984 as a result of chemical weapons use in the Iran-Iraq War. Made up of representatives from thirty nations, the group's goal is to limit the spread of chemical and biological weapons. They have created lists of materials and equipment that could be used to make BCW, which should be controlled. The group also lists items that if purchased by a nation might indicate weapons activities.

Thirty countries also make up the Nuclear Suppliers Group, which attempts to control nuclear exports. The group has set up guidelines for restricting the flow of nuclear technology and materials.

ARMS-CONTROL ORGANIZATIONS

Along with national governments and the United Nations, nongovernmental organizations (NGOs) are also working on ways to prevent the spread of WMD. The oldest, privately funded arms-control group in the United States is the Federation of American Scientists (FAS), located in Washington, D.C. Formerly the Federation of Atomic Scientists, FAS was founded in 1945 by scientists who produced the first atomic bomb. Today, its board includes forty-one Nobel Prize winners. FAS members provide expert testimony at congressional hearings on nonproliferation issues and maintain a Web site with extensive information on nuclear, chemical, and biological weapons and projects devoted to global security. One important project is FAS's Intelligence Resource Program that maintains a comprehensive list and descriptions of terrorist organizations and also reports on significant terrorist attacks around the world.[10]

The Henry L. Stimson Center also is based in Washington, D.C., and is named for the man who was secretary of war from 1940–1945. Stimson served both the Republican and Democratic administrations and was able to develop long-range public policy goals—which is the purpose of the Stimson Center. Not only does the center concern itself with diplomacy and military defense, but it also focuses on "economic, environmental, and demographic trends that will be critical to global stability in the decades ahead."[11]

Founded in 1971, the Arms Control Association (ACA) is another NGO that promotes public education and media programs on effective arms-control policies. The ACA also publishes *Arms Control Today*, which contains information on and analysis of arms-control proposals, negotiations, and agreements, as well as discussions on national security issues. In addition, ACA issues regular press briefings on major arms-control developments and provides commentary for journalists and scholars in the United States and other countries. ACA's Web site also provides background papers on arms-control agreements and other disarmament issues.[12]

Another NGO is the Chemical and Biological Arms Control Institute (CBACI), a nonprofit corporation established "to promote the goals of arms control and nonproliferation, with a special, although not exclusive focus on the elimination of chemical and biological weapons." CBACI works toward its goal through an extensive international network, developing research, analysis, technical support, and education on arms control.

The Center for Nonproliferation Studies (CNS) at the Monterey Institute of International Studies calls itself "the world's largest non-governmental organization devoted to combating the spread of weapons of mass destruction." CNS offices are located in Monterey, California; Washington, D.C.; and Almaty, Kazakhstan (once part of the Soviet Union). Through its journal, *The Nonproliferation Review*, CNS presents current research on arms control and also maintains a Web site that includes news on nonproliferation issues.[13]

An arms-control institute at Lancaster University in Great Britain is the Centre for Defence and International Security Studies (CDISS). CDISS research on defense and security matters apply not only to the United Kingdom but also to other parts of the world.[14]

In Sweden, the Stockholm International Peace Research Institute (SIPRI) has been at work since 1968 as an independent institute conducting research on peaceful solutions to international problems. The SIPRI investigates security issues, biological and chemical weapons, and other types of armaments. The institute also collects data on the development and transfer of weapons. Along with publishing numerous research reports, fact sheets, and books, the SIPRI issues an annual yearbook on *Armaments, Disarmament and International Security*, and maintains a Web site with links to other disarmament organizations.[15]

An important part of NGO activities is a campaign for an International Code of Conduct on Arms Transfers, which would be similar to codes that have been proposed in the United States and Great Britain. In the United States, a Code of Conduct Act would require the president to submit to Congress a list of countries that are eligible to import American arms. To qualify, a country is supposed to have a democratic form of government, respect its citizens' basic human rights, be nonaggressive toward other nations, and participate in the UN Register of Conventional Arms. Yet, Congress has not passed the Code of Conduct Act, and 85 percent of the countries that import U.S. weapons or arms equipment do not now meet the code standards.

CHAPTER 7
Future THREATS

In spite of the many arms-control agreements and efforts, biological, chemical, and nuclear weapons and their means of delivery will probably spread to nations or terrorist groups intent on mass destruction, warns the DOD. In the future, enemies of the United States likely will use "unconventional approaches to circumvent or undermine" U.S. strength. As a DOD report explains: "Strategically, an aggressor may seek to avoid direct confrontation with the United States, using instead terrorism, NBC threats, information warfare, or environmental sabotage to achieve its goals."[1]

Gathering information to gain advantage over the enemy has been an important part of warfare for centuries, but today and in the future, information technology and how information is used could change the way wars are conducted. Most command-and-control (C2) systems today are based on high-speed communication via computers. For example, during the first day of the Persian Gulf War in late 1990, electronic communications technology and information processing allowed the U.S. military to knock out Hussein's communications network and Baghdad's electrical power. During the following weeks, Americans watched TV films showing missiles streaking through the air guided by electronic information systems. Iraqi targets—from bridges to buildings—were destroyed with near perfect accuracy.

Nearly eight years later, after Iraq failed to keep its promise to allow UN inspectors to investigate sites where materials for biological and chemical weapons could be stored, U.S. and British forces launched Operation Desert Fox. While planes fired antiradar missiles at Iraqi defense posts, warships in the Persian Gulf launched hundreds of computer-guided cruise missiles, many more than were fired during the entire Gulf War. Cruise missiles were used rather than bombs dropped from airplanes because they present a lower risk to pilots, crews, and civilians on the ground. Targets that were hit included Iraqi military intelligence headquarters, air defense sites, radio and television transmitters, an oil production site, and facilities likely used to produce BCW.

Although the United States has been in a leading-edge position with its precision weapons, since the early 1990s many military experts, academics, and other professionals in the United States and allied countries have expressed concern that unfriendly nations can develop or already have developed sophisticated communications technology. The stage has been set for what is called information warfare, or infowar.

WHAT IS INFOWAR?

To some U.S. experts, infowar means protecting computers and other communications systems from the threat of an "electronic Pearl Harbor." But the surprise attack would not hit just one location, as was the case with the Japanese bombing of Pearl Harbor in Hawaii during World War II, but instead could disrupt the entire nation. Critical military databases, intelligence networks, satellite surveillance, air traffic-control systems, stock markets, railroad and shipping centers, sewage treatment plants, and other parts of the nation's infrastructure are controlled by or connected to computers and could be damaged or destroyed.

Other military experts define information warfare as not only defense against attacks but also offensive operations: achieving information superiority that allows a free flow of information with the ability to use it effectively but prevents an adversary from gaining the same capability.

How would that be done? Some analysts have discussed a variety of possible weapons, such as computer viruses that are fed into an adversary's computers to destroy files. One type of virus called a "logic bomb" could infect a computer system but not activate for weeks, months, or years; then if warfare breaks out an appropriate signal would trigger the "bomb" to attack the host system. A program called a "demon" or "sniffer" can be introduced into a system to record log-on information, passwords, and other data. Other types of computer programs could reproduce themselves over and over again and eventually destroy a system. Or a system could be designed so that someone with harmful intent could break in at a later date to, perhaps, interfere with military research and development, cut off satellite communications, or sabotage a banking system so that a nation appears to be on the verge of bankruptcy. Other information warfare devices are high-energy radio frequency (HERF) guns and electromagnetic pulse devices that can destroy electronics and communications equipment.

Yet these kinds of offensive weapons have major drawbacks. Antagonists can also use them. As the nonprofit RAND institution, which analyzes U.S. public policy and conducts ongoing research on the impact of information on the military, reported in 1996:

> The increasing availability of high-quality commercial communications, navigation, and surveillance information to virtually anyone who needs it—plus access to the Internet and other worldwide computer networks— may be a great equalizer in future "information wars." Almost anyone will be able to play, and denying access to "bad actors" may be difficult or impossible technically, politically, or legally.[2]

HOW VULNERABLE IS THE UNITED STATES?

In 1994 members of the U.S. Congress became alarmed when two teenage British hackers accessed the Air Force's command-and-control research center in Rome, New York. (In computerese, the term hackers at first referred to avid computer users, but now is often used as a synonym for computer users who are involved in theft, piracy, and fraud on the Internet.) The Rome break-ins prompted an investigation by the General Accounting Office (GAO) to assess the risks to military operations and national security. According to the GAO, only a small portion of attacks are ever detected, but the agency estimated that 250,000 intrusions had occurred in 1995.[3]

Although the 250,000 figure has been widely used to show how vulnerable military computers are, a report in the National Academy of Sciences journal, *Issues in Science and Technology*, maintains the total was highly exaggerated. The report, written by George Smith, an expert on computer security and information warfare, notes that the estimate of computer attacks was based on five hundred actual incidents and was multiplied by 0.2, which was believed to be the percentage of all possible intrusions. A computer scientist who led the investigation of the Air Force facility declared that the total number of intrusions was false, primarily because many of the attempts were "harmless probes," such as attempts to obtain addresses and telephone numbers of personnel.[4]

Smith sees no solid evidence that the nation is in danger of a major computer attack. However, he does not dismiss the fact that intrusions by hackers demonstrate the need for computer security. After all, in February 1998 two fourteen year olds in California gained access to Air Force, Army, and Navy logistical computers and installed programs that, if undiscovered, could have crashed the systems.

Earlier, in June 1997, the DOD had tested the security of its computers by conducting a secret war game called Eligible Receiver, attacking its own communication systems with software downloaded from Internet sites. Run over a two-week period, the game involved teams from the National Security Agency (NSA) who played the role of enemy hackers. The teams, who were stationed in Hawaii and other parts of the United States, gained access to the power grid that could have knocked out electricity throughout the nation. As *The Washington Times* reported, NSA hackers "floated effortlessly through global cyberspace, breaking into unclassified military computer networks in Hawaii, the headquarters of the U.S. Pacific Command, as well as in Washington, Chicago, St. Louis and parts of Colorado."

Although players in the war game did not actually shut down the power grid, their attack demonstrated once again how vulnerable electronic systems are. Even more telling was the team's intrusion and near takeover of the DOD's command-and-control center in the Pacific, which could have become inoperable for a lengthy period. In addition, the fake attackers were able to do their work without being detected. "FBI agents joined the Pentagon in trying to find the hackers, but for the most part they failed. Only one of the several NSA groups, a unit based in the United States, was uncovered. The rest operated without being located or identified."[5]

Computer security was the main focus of the Presidential Commission on Critical Infrastructure Protection (PCCIP) formed in 1996. For more than a year, the eighteen members of the commission from federal and state government and private industry and their staff investigated the nation's infrastructure. In a report issued in October 1997, the PCCIP declared that "our security, economy, way of life, and perhaps even survival, are now dependent on the interrelated trio of electrical energy, communications, and computers." Thus the nation is increasingly vulnerable. The commission found "no evidence of an impending cyber attack" and "no electronic disaster around the corner," but the "capability to do harm—particularly through information networks—is real; it is growing at an alarming rate, and we have little defense against it."[6]

A similar opinion was expressed by CIA Director George Tenet in mid-1998. According to *U.S. News & World Report*:

> In a closed briefing to Congress, the CIA chief said at least a dozen countries, some hostile to America, are developing programs to attack other nations' information and computer systems. China, Libya, Russia, Iraq, and Iran are among those deemed a threat. . . . Reflecting official thinking, no doubt, the *People's Liberation Daily* in China notes that a foe of the United States "only has to mess up the computer systems of its banks by hi-tech means. This would disrupt and destroy the U.S. economy."[7]

Even as warnings come from many quarters about the security of the nation's communications systems, there has been increasing awareness in both the public and private sectors of the need for infrastructure protection. The PCCIP recommends much broader programs of awareness and education, such as national conferences, presentations at industry associations and professional societies, development of elementary and secondary school materials, and graduate studies and programs. In addition, the commission recommends that research and development programs focus on new ways to detect and identify computer attacks and that "public and private sectors share responsibility for infrastructure protection."[8]

"REVOLUTION IN MILITARY AFFAIRS"

Secure and reliable information systems are a major component in what military planners in the United States (as well as other countries) call the Revolution in Military Affairs (RMA). This much-publicized revolution is based on the idea that information technologies and information processing are potent weapons. In a process that will take place until about 2010 or 2015, the U.S. military will "harness technology to ultimately bring about fundamental conceptual and organizational change," the DOD states.

Throughout history technological changes have had an impact on the way people fight and kill each other—going from arrows and spears to guns and bombs to nuclear, biological, and chemical weapons. But today "improved intelligence collection and assessment, as well as modern information processing and command and control capabilities, are at the heart of the military revolution currently under way," according to the DOD. In future warfare, C2 centers, rather than commanders, will be the chief targets, as they were in the Persian Gulf War and Operation Desert Fox.

The process of transforming the U.S. military is based on Joint Vision 2010 (JV 2010), concepts developed in the early 1990s by then Chairman of the Joint Chiefs of Staff General John Shalikashvili. These concepts, which can be accessed on the Internet and have been described in news articles, do not include military strategy or the makeup of armed forces. Instead they lay out a pattern for what is called "full spectrum dominance"—being superior in all aspects of warfare, including humanitarian aid. JV 2010 emphasizes teamwork that will "mass firepower without massing forces," decreasing the risk to troops through the use of improved information technology.

In other words, rather than bringing military troops together to strike an enemy's troops, "Massed forces will be replaced by massed firepower precisely placed on targets," as the Under Secretary of Defense for Acquisition and Technology Jacques Gansler explained. In a speech at the International Institute for Strategic Studies in Oxford, England, Gansler said that Revolution in Military Affairs

> is based on . . . accurate and secure information systems combined with long-range, unmanned, "brilliant", highly-lethal weapons designed to achieve precision kills. Technology has also enabled us to reduce dramatically our response time . . . . The type of regional conflict that we will see more frequently in the 21st century is likely not to allow six months to build up forces and deploy them . . . . Aggression will be instantaneous, with little warning, brutal, and difficult to defend against. This is particularly true in the case of . . . terrorist organizations—because they are willing to sacri-

fice themselves and their own civilian populations, as well as hostile civilian populations, to achieve their objectives. Our reaction to this form of aggression must be swift and decisive. The first few days, if not the first few hours, can easily determine the outcome. Our response must come within 24 hours . . . . Such responsiveness requires a significant change in doctrine, tactics, organization, and equipment.[9]

Will RMA actually be achieved? Critics certainly have their doubts, noting that the military has always been conservative and not eager to change. In addition, doubters wonder whether the different branches of the military and various agencies of the government can actually cooperate to bring about "full spectrum dominance." Another major question is where will the money come from to carry out the revolution?

Some skeptics also point to the fact that other nations—Russia and China, in particular—have their own RMA concepts and plans. The RMA has been widely discussed by military experts in China, according to Michael Pillsbury of the National Defense University. Pillsbury has translated at least two hundred Chinese military books and numerous articles, some of which are compiled in his book *Chinese Views of Future Warfare*.

Appearing before the U.S. Senate Select Committee on Intelligence in 1997, Pillsbury testified that since the late 1980s military experts in China have been examining how their country's future military capabilities could defeat the United States even though China is not equal in military power. One strategy is to employ the RMA more effectively and more rapidly than the United States.

The Chinese approach includes preemptive strikes—surprise attacks—to paralyze nerve centers and block logistics, Pillsbury testified. To do so, the Chinese experts advocate using "information-intensified" weapons and military units. In the Chinese view "information-intensified combat methods are like a Chinese boxer with a knowledge of vital body points who can bring an opponent to his knees with a minimum of movement."[10]

Many of the Chinese RMA concepts are similar to those of the United States. But U.S. defense planners are not certain whether China is actually modernizing its military. In fact, many experts believe just the opposite is true. Whatever the case, Pillsbury declared, the United States does not have "the necessary analytic tools and evidence" to know whether the Chinese military writings on RMA have any significance.[11]

INTELLIGENCE CAPABILITIES

Knowing what an adversary might and can do, backed up by evidence, is an important part of current and future security efforts in the United States. This requires exceptionally good intelligence in a number of areas, including surveillance, to determine who has and can deploy weapons. Because sneak attacks with nuclear, biological, or chemical weapons are the most likely kind of future warfare, detailed intelligence and warning systems will be needed for defense. If planned covert attacks are detected in advance, defense measures can be employed. As international security experts Falkenrath, Newman, and Thayer wrote:

> A ship with a nuclear weapon in the hold can be boarded, turned around, or sunk; a civilian aircraft with nuclear, biological, or chemical weapons on board can be shot down; a van with a biological aerosol sprayer in the back can be stopped, disarmed, and quarantined; a nerve gas canister in a building's air duct can be iso-

lated and contained, and the building evacuated; a terrorist with an improvised nerve gas dispenser in his backpack can be apprehended or shot.[12]

Of course, there is no guarantee that the United States will acquire enough information about a pending attack to mount a defense. And if ballistic missiles are used to deliver WMD, defense would be much more difficult. Nevertheless there have been numerous suggestions and recommendations for countering NBC terrorism and covert attacks. One would be to set up a center to conduct strategic planning for responding to NBC threats. Other recommendations call for:

- Reform and modernization of the U.S. intelligence community;

- Improvements in international intelligence cooperation;

- Increased intelligence to detect small-scale NBC programs;

- Increased and improved monitoring of diseases to determine whether a biological attack has occurred;

- Expansion of DOD efforts to train personnel who would respond to a large-scale biological or chemical attack.[13]

Other suggestions include:

- Increased funding for research on detecting and diminishing the effects of WMD;
- Increased prevention efforts to stop the "brain drain" of Russian weapons scientists to countries hostile to the United States;
- Improved protection for U.S. and foreign borders to detect WMD at entry points.[14]

Many insist that the basic goal should be arms control—stopping the spread of biological, chemical, and nuclear weapons. That was part of the rationale for the American-British attack on Iraq in December 1998. Beyond bombings, however, many peace and arms-control groups call for increased efforts to implant a widespread moral disgust for weapons of mass destruction. The production, storage, and deployment of weapons that can secretly and silently cause deaths on a massive scale must be seen on an international scale as ethically wrong—a hated evil.

SOURCE NOTES

Chapter 1

1. Thomas V. Inglesby, "Anthrax: A Possible Case History," *Emerging Infectious Diseases*, July–August 1999, p. 556.
2. Mayo Health Oasis, "Anthrax: Ancient Disease Turned Biological Weapon," Mayo Foundation for Medical Education and Research, February 20, 1998, on the Internet. http://www.mayohealth.org/cgi-bin/iatoc.bln
3. Ellen Walterscheid, "Ill Wind: Living With the Threat of Biological Terrorism," *The Sciences*, March–April 1998 (electronic version).
4. Jessica Stern, *The Ultimate Terrorists*, Cambridge, MA: Harvard University Press, 1999, p.27.
5. Daniel Klaidman and Evan Thomas, "Americans on Alert," *Newsweek*, January 1, 2000, pp. 10–13.
6. Avigdor Haselkorn, *The Continuing Storm: Iraq, Poisonous Weapons, and Deterrence*, New Haven and London: Yale University Press, 1999, p. 16.
7. Barton Gellman and Dana Priest, "U.S. Strikes Terrorist-Linked Sites in Afghanistan, Factory in Sudan," *The Washington Post*, August 21, 1998, p. A1. Also Tim Weiner, "Afghan Camps, Hidden in Hills, Stymied Soviet Attacks for Years," *The New York Times*, August 24, 1998, p. A1.

8. Quoted in Jose Vegar, "Terrorism's New Breed," *Bulletin of the Atomic Scientists*, March–April 1998 (electronic version).
9. President Bill Clinton, "Terror Has Become the World's Problem," excerpts from White House transcript, *The Washington Post*, September 22, 1998, p. A13.

Chapter 2

1. Office of Senator Jay Rockefeller, "DOD Acknowledges for the First Time That Potentially Dangerous Drug Was Used Improperly in Persian Gulf War," Press Release, March 17, 1998.
2. Leonard A. Cole, *The Eleventh Plague: The Politics of Biological and Chemical Warfare*, New York: W. H. Freeman and Company, 1997, p. 158.
3. Quoted in John M. Blum, Bruce Catton, Edmund S. Morgan, Arthur M. Schlesinger Jr., Kenneth M. Stampp, and C. Vann Woodward, *The National Experience, Part Two*, New York: Harcourt, Brace and World, 1968, p. 596.
4. Jessica Stern, *The Ultimate Terrorists*, Cambridge, MA: Harvard University Press, 1999, p. 25.
5. Quoted in News Bureau Medical College of Georgia, "MCG Studying Effects of Chemical Warfare Agents," News Release, April 21, 1995, *MCG Today*, Fall 1995, on the Internet.
   http://www.mcg.edu/News/95NewsRel/GulfWar.html
6. Ibid.
7. Swedish Defence Research Establishment, *FOA Briefing Book on Chemical Weapons*, 1992, on the Internet.
   http://www.opcw.nl/chemhaz/nerve.htm
8. Christine Gosden, "Why I Went, What I Saw," *The Washington Post*, March 11, 1998, p. A19.
9. Organization for the Prohibition of Chemical Weapons, "Dispersal of Chemical Warfare Agents" from the *FOA Briefing Book on Chemical Weapons*, on the Internet.
   http://www.opcw.nl/chemhaz/disperse.htm
10. Ibid.

Chapter 3

1. "Status of Verification of Iraq's Biological Warfare Programme UNSCOM—Report to the Security Council, January 25, 1999, on the Internet. http://www.fas.org/news/un/iraq/s/990125/dis-bio.htm
2. Quoted in Reuters, "Former Inspector: Iraq Hiding Arms Capabilities Abroad," *San Jose Mercury News*, August 27, 1998 (electronic version).
3. "The Iraq Situation, Will Saddam Hussein Comply with the Latest Agreement?" *Online NewsHour*, February 27, 1998, transcript on the Internet. http://www.pbs.org/newshour/forum/february98/iraq2.htm
4. John D. Steinbruner, "Biological Weapons: A Plague Upon All Houses," *Foreign Policy*, Winter 1997–98, (electronic version).
5. Graham S. Pearson, in the Henry L. Stimson Center Report No. 24, *Biological Weapons Proliferation: Reasons for Concern, Courses of Action*, "The Threat of Deliberate Disease in the 21st Century," January 1998, on the Internet. http://www.brad.ac.uk/acad/sbtwc/other/disease.htm
6. Richard Norton-Taylor, "Anthrax Bomb Tests Were 'Playing with Fire,'" *The Guardian*, July 21, 1999. Also Neil Tweedie, "Girls Worked in Germ War Labs," *The Daily Telegraph*, July 21, 1999.
7. Leonard A. Cole, *The Eleventh Plague: The Politics of Biological and Chemical Warfare*, New York: W. H. Freeman and Company, 1997, pp. 18–19.
8. Richard A. Falkenrath, Robert D. Newman, and Bradley A. Thayer, *America's Achilles' Heel: Nuclear, Biological, and Chemical Terrorism and Covert Attack*, Cambridge, MA: MIT Press, 1998, p. 33.
9. Richard Danzig and Pamela B. Berkowsky, "Why Should We Be Concerned About Biological Warfare?" *The Journal of the American Medical Association*, August 6, 1997, p. 431.

10. U.S. Department of Health and Human Services, "HHS Initiative Prepares for Possible Bioterrorism Threat," Fact Sheet, October 12, 1999, on the Internet. http://www.hhs.gov/news/press/1999pres/991012b.html

11. Lt. Col. Robert P. Kadlec, USAF, M.D., "Biological Weapons for Waging Economic Warfare," in Barry R. Schneider and Lawrence E. Grinter, eds., *Battlefield of the Future: 21st Century Warfare Issues*, Maxwell Air Force Base, Alabama: Air War College Studies in National Security, 1995, Chapter 10. http://www.airpower.maxwell.af.mil/airchronicles/battle/chp10.html

12. Ibid.

13. Judith Miller and William J. Broad, "Germ Weapons: In Soviet Past or in the New Russia's Future?" *The New York Times*, December 28, 1998 (electronic version), p. A1.

14. Ibid.

15. Ken Alibek with Stephen Handelman, *Biohazard*, New York: Random House, 1999, p. x.

16. Ibid., p. 292.

17. John D. Steinbruner, "Biological Weapons: A Plague Upon All Houses," *Foreign Policy*, Winter 1997–98 (electronic version).

18. Quoted in Graham S. Pearson, in the Henry L. Stimson Center Report No. 24, *Biological Weapons Proliferation: Reasons for Concern, Courses of Action*, "The Threat of Deliberate Disease in the 21st Century," January 1998, on the Internet. http://www.brad.ac.uk/acad/sbtwc/other/disease.htm

19. Quoted in William J. Broad and Judith Miller, "Once He Devised Germ Weapons; Now He Defends Against Them," *The New York Times*, November 3, 1998 (electronic version), p. F1.

20. Zachary Selden, "Report Update. Biological Weapons: Defense Improves, But the Threat Remains," Washington, D.C.: BENS Special Report, 1997, on the Internet. http://www.bens.org/pubs/bioup.html

21. Richard Danzig, "The Next Superweapon: Panic," *The New York Times*, November 15, 1998, Op-Ed, IV, 15.

22. Jessica Stern, "The Prospect of Domestic Bioterrorism," *Emerging Infectious Diseases*, July–August 1999 (electronic version), p. 517.

Chapter 4

1. Ely Karmon, "Intelligence and the Challenge of Terrorism in the 21st Century," paper presented at the conference, A Counter-Terrorism Strategy for the 21st Century: The Role of Intelligence, Tel Aviv University, November 1–2, 1998, on the Internet. http://www.counterror.org.il/articles/articledet.cfm?articleid=54

2. U.S. State Department Office of Coordinator for Counterterrorism, "Patterns of Global Terrorism: 1998, Year in Review," April 1999, on the Internet. http://www.state.gov/www/global/terrorism/1998Report/review.html.

3. ADL Backgrounder, "Osama bin Laden," August 20, 1998 on the Internet. http://www.adl.org/frames/front_backgrounders.html

4. "The 'War of the Future,'" Editorial, *The Nation*, September 21, 1998, pp. 6–7.

5. Robert Fisk, "Talks With Osama bin Laden: How an Afghan 'Freedom Fighter' Became 'America's Public Enemy Number One,'" *The Nation*, September 21, 1998, pp. 24–27.

6. Quoted in Caspar W. Weinberger, "Long-overdue Attack on Terrorism," *Forbes*, September 21, 1998, p. 41.

7. C. L. Staten, "International Terrorism; Where Do We Go From Here?" August 31, 1998, on the Internet. http://www.emergency.com/ennday.htm

8. Steven Pomerantz, "Counterterrorism in a Free Society," *The Journal of Counterterrorism & Security International*, Spring 1998, on the Internet. http://MSA.News.Mynet.net/MSANEWS/199806/19990626.0.html

9. Boaz Ganor, "Countering State-Sponsored Terrorism," April 25, 1998, on the Internet. http://www.counterror.org.il/articles/articledet.cfm?articleid=5

10. U.S. State Department Office of Coordinator for Counter-terrorism, "Foreign Terrorist Organizations," Designations by Secretary of State Madeleine K. Albright, October 8, 1999, on the Internet.
http://www.state.gov/www/global/terrorism/fto_1999.html
11. ADL Online, "ADL Files Amicus Brief in Support of Antiterrorism Act," *Terrorism Update*, Fall 1998, on the Internet.
http://www.adl.org/frames/front_search.html
12. ADL Online, "Counterterrorism Abroad," *Terrorism Update*, Fall 1998, on the Internet.
http://www.adl.org/frames/front_terrorism_up.html
13. U.S. State Department Office of Coordinator for Counter-terrorism, "International Terrorism Conventions," August 17, 1998, on the Internet.
http://www.state.gov/www/global/terrorism/980817_terror_conv.html
14. Judith Miller with William J. Broad, "Dollar Is Weapon of Choice in War on Bacterial Perils," *The New York Times*, December 8, 1998, p. A12.
15. U.S. Department of Defense, "1997 Annual Defense Report," Chapter 9, on the Internet.
http://www.dtic.mil/execsec/adr97/chap9.html

Chapter 5

1. Joan Stephenson, "Pentagon-Funded Research Takes Aim at Agents of Biological Warfare," *Journal of the American Medical Association*, August 6, 1997, pp. 373–375.
2. Clark L. Staten, "Emergency Response to Chemical/Biological Terrorist Incidents,"*ERRI Lessons on Line*, August 7, 1997, on the Internet.
http://205.243.133.2/cbwlesn1.htm
3. Richard Danzig, "The Next Superweapon: Panic," *The New York Times*, November 15, 1998 , Op-Ed, IV, 15.
4. Lois R. Ember, "FBI Takes Lead in Developing Counterter-rorism Effort," *Chemical & Engineering News*, November 4, 1996, pp. 10–16.

5. Ibid.
6. U.S. Department of Defense, News Release, "Remarks Prepared for Delivery by U.S. Secretary of Defense William S. Cohen, Council on Foreign Relations New York, New York," September 14, 1998, on the Internet. http://www.defenselink.mil/news/Sep1998/
7. Ibid.
8. Bradley Graham, "Anti-Terrorism Plans Termed Inadequate," *The Washington Post*, October 3, 1998, p. A9.
9. Alesia Stanford, "Scientists Testing New Detector for Chemical Agents," CNN Web post, February 20, 1998. http://www3.cnn.com/TECH/science/9802/20/chemical. weapons
10. Ken Alibek with Stephen Handelman, *Biohazard*, New York: Random House, 1999, p. 19; also Wendy Orent, "Escape From Moscow," *The Sciences*, May–June 1998 (electronic version).
11. Debra MacKenzie, "Bioarmageddon," Bioterrorism Special Report, *New Scientist*, September 11, 1998, on the Internet. http://www.newscientist.com/nsplus/insight/ bioterrorism/bioarmageddon.html
12. Quoted in Judith Miller and William J. Broad, "Germ Weapons: In Soviet Past or in the New Russia's Future?" *The New York Times*, December 28, 1998 (electronic version).

Chapter 6

1. "Text of Clinton Letter on Weapons of Mass Destruction," White House press release, November 12, 1998.
2. Secretary of State Albright, "Arms Control in the 21st Century," transcript of remarks at the Stimson Center Forum on South Asia, June 10, 1998, on the Internet. http://www.stimson.org/ndanger/albright.htm
3. Raymond A. Zilinskas, "Verifying Compliance to the Biological and Toxin Weapons Convention," excerpts *Critical Reviews in Microbiology*, Special Issue: Biological Weapons, Vol. 24, Issue 3, 1998, on the Internet. http://cns.miis.edu/pubs/reports/bwcverif.htm

4. Arms Control and Defense Agency, "The Chemical Weapons Convention," fact sheet, September 1998, on the Internet.
http://dosfan.lib.uic.edu/acda/

5. Organisation for the Prohibition of Chemical Weapons, "A Guided Tour of the Convention on the Prohibition of the Development, Production, Stockpiling and Use of Chemical Weapons and on Their Destruction," September 1998, on the Internet.
http://www.opcw.nl/

6. "Treaty on the Non-Proliferation of Nuclear Weapons," 1968, on the Internet.
http://dosfan.lib.uic.edu/acda/

7. Richard A. Falkenrath, Robert D. Newman, and Bradley A. Thayer, *America's Achilles' Heel: Nuclear, Biological, and Chemical Terrorism and Covert Attack*, Cambridge, MA: MIT Press, 1998, pp. 63–66.

8. Arms Control and Disarmament Agency Fact Sheet, "U.S. Commitment to the Treaty on Non-Proliferation of Nuclear Weapons," April 22, 1998, on the Internet.
http://dosfan.lib.uic.edu/acda/factshee/wmd/nuclear/

9. Quoted in Arms Control and Disarmament Agency Fact Sheet, March 27, 1998, on the Internet.
http://dosfan.lib.uic.edu/acda/

10. See http://www.fas.org/about.htm

11. See http://www.stimson.org/stimson/mission.htm

12. See http://www.armscontrol.org/home.htm

13. See http://cns.miis.edu/news/other/wmdlet.htm

14. See http://www.cdiss.org/hometemp.htm

15. See http://www.sipri.se/

Chapter 7

1. U.S. Department of Defense, "1998 Annual Defense Report," Chapter 1, on the Internet.
http://www.dtic.mil/execsec/adr98/chap1.html

2. Glenn Buchan, "Information War and the Air Force: Wave of the Future? Current Fad?" March 1996, on the Internet.
http://www.rand.org/publications/IP/IP149/

3. General Accounting Office, "Information Security—Computer Attacks at Department of Defense Pose Increasing Risks," May 1996, on the Internet. http://www.epic.org/security/GAO_DOD_security.html

4. George Smith, "An Electronic Pearl Harbor? Not Likely," *Issues in Science and Technology*, Fall 1998, on the Internet. http://205.130.85.236/issues/15.1/smith.htm

5. Bill Gertz, "Eligible Receiver," *The Washington Times*, April 16, 1998 (electronic version).

6. President's Commission on Critical Infrastructure Protection, "Critical Foundations: Protecting America's Infrastructures," October 1997, summary on the Internet. http://www.pccip.gov/summary.html; full report http://www.pccip.gov/report.pdf

7. Douglas Pasternak and Bruce B. Auster, "Terrorism at the Touch of a Keyboard," *U.S. News & World Report*, July 13, 1998, p. 37.

8. President's Commission on Critical Infrastructure Protection, "Critical Foundations: Protecting America's Infrastructures," October 1997, summary on the Internet. http://www.pccip.gov/summary.html; full report http://www.pccip.gov/report.pdf

9. Jacques S. Gansler, "Technology and Future Warfare," September 3, 1998, on the Internet. http://www.acq.osd.mil/ousda/speech/oxford.html

10. Quoted in Michael Pillsbury "Chinese Views of Future Warfare: Implications for the Intelligence Community," transcript of testimony before the United States Senate Select Committee on Intelligence Hearing, September 18, 1997, *Miami Herald*, September 29, 1997 (electronic version).

11. Ibid.

12. Richard A. Falkenrath, Robert D. Newman, and Bradley A. Thayer, *America's Achilles' Heel: Nuclear, Biological, and Chemical Terrorism and Covert Attack*, Cambridge, MA: MIT Press, 1998, p. 249.

13. Ibid., Chapter 5.

14. Jessica Stern, *The Ultimate Terrorists*, Cambridge, MA: Harvard University Press, 1999, Chapter 8.

FURTHER INFORMATION

BOOKS

Alibek, Ken with Stephen Handelman. *Biohazard: The Chilling True Story of the Largest Covert Biological Weapons Program in the World—Told from Inside by the Man Who Ran it.* New York: Random House, 1999.

Cole, Leonard A. *The Eleventh Plague: The Politics of Biological and Chemical Warfare.* New York: W.H. Freeman and Company, 1997.

Haselkorn, Avigdor. *The Continuing Storm: Iraq, Poisonous Weapons, and Deterrence.* New Haven and London: Yale University Press, 1999.

Hersh, Seymour M. *Against All Enemies Gulf War Syndrome: The War Between America's Ailing Veterans and Their Government.* New York: Ballantine, 1998.

Hoffman, Bruce. *Inside Terrorism.* New York: Columbia University Press, 1998.

Mauroni, Albert J. *America's Struggle with Chemical-Biological Warfare.* New York: Praeger, 2000.

Pringle, Laurence. *Chemical and Biological Warfare: The Cruelest Weapons* (Revised Edition). Berkeley Heights, NJ: Enslow Publishers, 2000.

Regis, Ed. *The Biology of Doom: The History of America's Secret Germ Warfare Project.* New York: Henry Holt, 1999.

Stern, Jessica. *The Ultimate Terrorists.* Cambridge, MA: Harvard University Press, 1999.

SELECTED WEB SITES

Air Chronicles
http://airpower.maxwell.af.mil/airchronicles

Arms Control Association
http://www.armscontrol.org

Bradford-SIPRI Project on Strengthening the Biological and Toxin Weapons Convention and Preventing Biological Warfare
http://www.brad.ac.uk/acad/sbtwc/

Business Executives for National Security
http://www.bens.org

Center for Strategic & International Studies
http://www.csis.org

Centers for Disease Control and Prevention
http://www.cdc.gov

Centre for Defence and International Security
http://www.cdiss.org

Chemical and Biological Arms Control Institute
http://www.cbaci.org

Emerging Infectious Diseases
http://www.cdc.gov/ncidod/EID/

Federation of American Scientists
http://www.fas.org

Henry L. Stimson Center
http://www.stimson.org

Journal of the American Medical Association
http://www.ama-assn.org/public/journals/jama/jamahome.htm

Monterey Institute of International Studies Center for Non-proliferation Studies
http://cns.miis.edu

National Institutes of Health
http://www.nih.gov

Organization for the Prohibition of Chemical Weapons
http://www.opcw.nl

Political Terrorism Database
http://polisci.home.mindspring.com/ptd_incidents.html

PREEMPT
http://home.eznet.net/~kenberry

Stockholm International Peace Research Institute
http://www.sipri.se/

United States Arms Control and Disarmament Agency
http://dosfan.lib.uic.edu/acda.link/htm

United States Army Soldier and Biological Chemical Command
http://www.cbdcom.apgea.army.mil/

United States Department of Defense
http://www.defenselink.mil

United States Department of Health and Human Services
http://www.dhhs.gov

United States Department of State
http://www.state.gov

United States General Accounting Office
http://www.gao.gov

Vietnam Veterans Home Page
http://grunt.space.swri.edu

APPENDIX A TABLE OF

Agent	Onset	Symptoms & Effects	Treatment
		B A C T E R I A	
Bacillus anthracis (causes anthrax)	1–6 days	Fever, fatigue, severe respiratory problems, shock, pneumonia and death within 2–3 days	Early treatment with antibiotics Preventive measure: vaccine
Yersinia pestis (causes plague)	2–10 days	Malaise, high fever, tender lymph nodes, possible bleeding, circulatory failure, and death	Antibiotics have to be given within 24 hours of onset of symptoms
Pasturella tularensis (causes tularemia)	2–4 days	Fever, headache, general discomfort, cough, exhaustion	Antibiotics must be given early
		R I C K E T T S I A	
Coxiella burnetti (causes Q fever)	15–18 days	Aches, fever, cough	Treatable with antibiotics

BIOLOGICAL AND CHEMICAL AGENTS

VIRUSES

Flaviviridae (yellow fever)	3–15 days	Severe headache and fever, vomiting, muscle/joint pain, bleeding	No specific treatment exists; vaccine available
Venezuelan equine encephalitis	2–5 days	Chills, headache, joint pain, vomiting, diarrhea	No specific treatment exists; vaccine available

TOXINS

Clostridium botulinum (botulinum toxin)	24–36 hours	Weakness, dizziness, vomiting, blurred vision, abrupt respiratory failure	Must treat early with antitoxin
Ricin (from castor beans)	18–24 hours	Nausea, vomiting, cramps, severe respiratory distress, cough	No treatment available
Staphylococcus aureus (staphylococcal enterotoxin B; staph infection)	3–12 hours	Severe nausea, diarrhea, vomiting	No specific treatment

APPENDIX B
Foreign
TERRORIST
Organizations

Foreign Terrorist Organizations, U.S. Department of State
Background Information on Foreign Terrorist Organizations
Released by the Office of Counterterrorism, October 8, 1999:

Abu Nidal Organization (ANO) a.k.a. Black September, the Fatah Revolutionary Council, the Arab Revolutionary Council, the Arab Revolutionary Brigades, the Revolutionary Organization of Socialist Muslims

Description: International terrorist organization led by Sabri al-Banna. Split from PLO in 1974. Made up of various functional committees, including political, military, and financial.

Activities: Has carried out terrorist attacks in twenty countries, killing or injuring almost nine hundred persons. Targets include the United States, the United Kingdom, France, Israel, moderate Palestinians, the PLO, and various Arab countries. Major attacks included the Rome and Vienna airports in December 1985, the Neve Shalom Synagogue in Istanbul, the Pan Am Flight 73 hijacking in Karachi in September 1986, and the City of Poros day-excursion ship attack in July 1988 in Greece. Suspected of assassinating PLO deputy chief Abu Iyad and PLO security chief Abu Hu l in Tunis in January 1991. ANO assassinated a Jordanian diplomat in Lebanon in January 1994 and has been linked to the killing of the PLO representative there. Has not attacked Western targets since the late 1980s.

Strength: Several hundred plus militia in Lebanon and limited overseas support structure.

Location/Area of Operation: Al-Banna may have relocated to Iraq in December 1998, where the group maintains a presence. Has an operational presence in Lebanon in the Bekaa Valley and several Palestinian refugee camps in coastal areas of Lebanon. Also has a presence in Sudan and Syria, among others. Has demonstrated ability to operate over wide area, including the Middle East, Asia, and Europe.

External Aid: Has received considerable support, including safe haven, training, logistic assistance, and financial aid from Iraq, Libya, and Syria (until 1987), in addition to close support for selected operations.

Abu Sayyaf Group (ASG) a.k.a. Al Harakat Al Islamiyy

Description: Smallest and most radical of the Islamic separatist groups operating in the southern Philippines. Split from the Moro National Liberation Front in 1991 under the leadership of Abdurajik Abubakar Janjalani, who was killed in a clash with Philippine police on December 18, 1998. Some members have studied or worked in the Middle East and developed ties to Arab mujahideen while fighting and training in Afghanistan.

Activities: Uses bombs, assassinations, kidnappings, and extortion payments to promote an independent Islamic state in western Mindanao and the Sulu Archipelago, areas in the southern Philippines heavily populated by Muslims. Raided the town of Ipil in Mindanao in April 1995, the group's first large-scale action. Suspected of several small-scale bombings and kidnappings in 1998.

Strength: Unknown, but believed to have about two hundred members.

Location/Area of Operation: The ASG operates in the southern Philippines and occasionally in Manila.

External Aid: Probably receives support from Islamic extremists in the Middle East and South Asia.

Armed Islamic Group (GIA) a.k.a. Groupement Islamique Arme, AIG, Al-Jama'ah al-Islamiyah al-Musallah

Description: An Islamic extremist group, the GIA aims to overthrow the secular Algerian regime and replace it with an Islamic state. The GIA began its violent activities in early 1992 after Algiers voided the victory of the Islamic Salvation Front (FIS)—the largest Islamic party—in the first round of legislative elections in December 1991.

Activities: Frequent attacks against civilians, journalists, and foreign residents. In the last several years the GIA has conducted a terrorist campaign of civilian massacres, sometimes wiping out entire villages in its area of operations and frequently killing hundreds of civilians. Since announcing its terrorist campaign against foreigners living in Algeria in September 1993, the GIA has killed more than one hundred expatriate men and women—mostly Europeans—in the country. Uses assassinations and bombings, including car bombs, and it is known to favor kidnapping victims and slitting their throats. The GIA hijacked an Air France flight to Algiers in December 1994, and suspicions centered on the group for a series of bombings in France in 1995.

Strength: Unknown, probably between several hundred and several thousand.

Location/Area of Operation: Algeria.

External Aid: Algerian expatriates and GIA members abroad, many of whom reside in Western Europe, provide some financial and logistic support. In addition, the Algerian government has accused Iran and Sudan of supporting Algerian extremists and severed diplomatic relations with Iran in March 1993.

Aum Shinrikyo (a.k.a. Aum Supreme Truth, A.I.C. Sogo Kenkyusho, A.I.C. Comprehensive Research Institute)

Description: A cult established in 1987 by Shoko Asahara, Aum aims to take over Japan and then the world. Its organizational structure mimics that of a nation-state, with "finance, construction, and science and technology" ministries. Approved as a religious entity in 1989 under Japanese law, the group ran candidates in a Japanese parliamentary election in 1990. Over time, the cult began to emphasize the imminence of the end of the world and stated that the United States would initiate "Armageddon" by starting World War III with Japan. The Japanese government revoked its recognition of Aum as a religious organization in October 1995, but in 1997 a government panel decided not to invoke the Anti-Subversive Law against the group, which would have outlawed the cult.

Activities: On March 20, 1995, Aum members simultaneously released sarin nerve gas on several Tokyo subway trains, killing twelve persons and injuring up to six thousand. The group was responsible for other mysterious chemical incidents in Japan in 1994. Its efforts to conduct attacks using biological agents have been unsuccessful. Japanese police arrested Asahara in May 1995, and he remained on trial facing seventeen counts of murder at the beginning of 2000. In 1997 and 1998 the cult resumed its recruiting activities in Japan and opened several commercial businesses. Maintains an Internet home page that indicates Armageddon and anti-U.S. sentiment remain a part of the cult's world view.

Strength: At the time of the Tokyo subway attack, the group claimed to have 9,000 members in Japan and up to 40,000 worldwide. Its current strength is unknown.

Location/Area of Operation: Operates in Japan, but previously had a presence in Australia, Russia, Ukraine, Germany, Taiwan, Sri Lanka, the former Yugoslavia, and the United States.

External Aid: None.

Basque Fatherland and Liberty (ETA)
a.k.a Euzkadi Ta Askatasuna

Description: Founded in 1959 with the aim of establishing an independent homeland based on Marxist principles in Spain's Basque region and the southwestern French provinces of Labourd, Basse-Navarra, and Soule.

Activities: Primarily bombings and assassinations of Spanish government officials, especially security and military forces, politicians, and judicial figures. In response to French operations against the group, ETA also has targeted French interests. Finances its activities through kidnappings, robberies, and extortion. Has killed more than eight hundred persons since it began lethal attacks in the early 1960s; responsible for murdering six persons in 1998. ETA declared a "unilateral and indefinite" cease-fire on September 17, 1998.

Strength: Unknown; may have several hundred members, plus supporters.

Location/Area of Operation: Operates primarily in the Basque autonomous regions of northern Spain and southwestern France, but also has bombed Spanish and French interests elsewhere in the world.

External Aid: Has received training at various times in the past in Libya, Lebanon, and Nicaragua. Some ETA members allegedly have received sanctuary in Cuba. Also appears to have ties to the Irish Republican Army through the legal political wings of the two groups.

Gama'a al-Islamiyya (the Islamic Group, IG) a.k.a. al-Gama'at, Islamic Gama'at, Egyptian al-Gama'at al-Islamiyya, GI

Description: Egypt's largest militant group, active since the late 1970s; appears to be loosely organized. Has an external wing with a worldwide presence. Signed Osama bin Ladin's fatwa in February 1998 calling for attacks against U.S. civilians but publicly has denied that it supports bin Ladin. Shaykh Umar Abd al-Rahman is al-Gama'at's preeminent spiritual leader, and the group publicly has threatened to retaliate against U.S. interests for his incarceration. Primary goal is to overthrow the Egyptian government and replace it with an Islamic state.

Activities: Armed attacks against Egyptian security and other government officials, Coptic Christians, and Egyptian opponents of Islamic extremism. Al-Gama'at has launched attacks on tourists in Egypt since 1992, most notably the attack in November 1997 at Luxor that killed fifty-eight foreign tourists. Also claimed responsibility for the attempt in June 1995 to assassinate Egyptian President Hosni Mubarak in Addis Ababa, Ethiopia.

Strength: Unknown, but probably several thousand hard-core members and another several thousand sympathizers.

Location/Area of Operation: Operates mainly in the Al Minya, Asyu't, Qina, and Soha governorates of southern Egypt. Also appears to have support in Cairo, Alexandria, and other urban locations, particularly among unemployed graduates and students. Has a worldwide presence, including in the United Kingdom, Afghanistan, and Austria.

External Aid: Unknown. The Egyptian government believes that Iranian, Sudanese, and Afghan militant groups support the IG.

HAMAS (Islamic Resistance Movement) a.k.a. Harakat al-Muqawama al-Islamiya, Students of Ayyash, Students of the Engineer, Yahya Ayyash Units, Izz Al-Din Al-Qassim Brigades, Izz Al-Din Al-Qassim Forces, Izz Al-Din Al-Qassim Battalions, Izz al-Din Al Qassam Brigades, Izz al-Din Al Qassam Forces, Izz al-Din Al Qassam Battalions

Description: Formed in late 1987 as an outgrowth of the Palestinian branch of the Muslim Brotherhood. Various HAMAS elements have used both political and violent means, including terrorism, to pursue the goal of establishing an Islamic Palestinian state in place of Israel. Loosely structured, with some elements working clandestinely and others working openly through mosques and social-service institutions to recruit members, raise money, organize activities, and distribute propaganda. HAMAS's strength is concentrated in the Gaza Strip and a few areas of the West Bank. Also has engaged in peaceful political activity, such as running candidates in West Bank Chamber of Commerce elections.

Activities: HAMAS activists, especially those in the Izz el-Din al-Qassam Brigades, have conducted many attacks—including large-scale suicide bombings—against Israeli civilian and military targets, suspected Palestinian collaborators, and Fatah rivals.

Strength: Unknown number of hard-core members; tens of thousands of supporters and sympathizers.

Location/Area of Operation: Primarily the occupied territories, Israel, and Jordan.

External Aid: Receives funding from Palestinian expatriates, Iran, and private benefactors in Saudi Arabia and other moderate Arab states. Some fund-raising and propaganda activity take place in Western Europe and North America.

Harakat ul-Mujahideen (HUM) a.k.a. Harakat ul-Ansar, HUA, Al-Hadid, Al-Hadith, Al-Faran

Description: Formerly the Harakat ul-Ansar, which was designated a foreign terrorist organization in October 1997. HUM is an Islamic militant group based in Pakistan that operates primarily in Kashmir. Leader Fazlur Rehman Khalil has been linked to bin Ladin and signed his fatwa in February 1998 calling for attacks on U.S. and Western interests. Operates terrorist training camps in eastern Afghanistan and suffered casualties in the U.S. missile strikes on bin Ladin-associated training camps in Khowst in August 1998. Fazlur Rehman Khalil subsequently said that HUM would take revenge on the United States.

Activities: Has conducted a number of operations against Indian troops and civilian targets in Kashmir. Linked to the Kashmiri militant group al-Faran that kidnapped five Western tourists in Kashmir in July 1995; one was killed in August 1995, and the other four reportedly were killed in December of the same year.

Strength: Has several thousand armed supporters located in Azad Kashmir, Pakistan, and India's southern Kashmir and Doda regions. Supporters are mostly Pakistanis and Kashmiris, and also include Afghans and Arab veterans of the Afghan war. Uses light and heavy machine guns, assault rifles, mortars, explosives, and rockets.

Location/Area of Operation: Based in Muzaffarabad, Pakistan, but members conduct insurgent and terrorist activities primarily in Kashmir. The HUM trains its militants in Afghanistan and Pakistan.

External Aid: Collects donations from Saudi Arabia and other Gulf and Islamic states and from Pakistanis and Kashmiris. The source and amount of HUA's military funding are unknown.

Hizballah (Party of God) a.k.a. Islamic Jihad, Islamic Jihad Organization, Revolutionary Justice Organization, Organization of the Oppressed on Earth, Islamic Jihad for the Liberation of Palestine, Organization of Right Against Wrong, Ansar Allah, Followers of the Prophet Muhammed

Description: Radical Shia group formed in Lebanon; dedicated to creation of Iranian-style Islamic republic in Lebanon and removal of all non-Islamic influences from the area. Strongly anti-West and anti-Israel. Closely allied with, and often directed by, Iran but may have conducted operations that were not approved by Tehran.

Activities: Known or suspected to have been involved in numerous anti-U.S. terrorist attacks, including the suicide truck bombing of the U.S. Embassy and U.S. Marine barracks in Beirut in October 1983 and the U.S. Embassy annex in Beirut in September 1984. Elements of the group were responsible for the kidnapping and detention of U.S. and other Western hostages in Lebanon. The group also attacked the Israeli Embassy in Argentina in 1992.

Strength: Several thousand.

Location/Area of Operation: Operates in the Bekaa Valley, the southern suburbs of Beirut, and southern Lebanon. Has established cells in Europe, Africa, South America, North America, and elsewhere.

External Aid: Receives substantial amounts of financial, training, weapons, explosives, political, diplomatic, and organizational aid from Iran and Syria.

Japanese Red Army (JRA) a.k.a. Anti-Imperialist International Brigade (AIIB), Nippon Sekigun, Nihon Sekigun, the Holy War Brigade, the Antiwar Democratic Front

Description: An international terrorist group formed around 1970 after breaking away from Japanese Communist League-

Red Army Faction. Led by Fusako Shigenobu, believed to be in Syrian-garrisoned area of Lebanon's Bekaa Valley. Stated goals are to overthrow Japanese government and monarchy and help foment world revolution. Organization unclear but may control or at least have ties to Anti-Imperialist International Brigade (AIIB). Also may have links to Antiwar Democratic Front, an overt leftist political organization in Japan. Details released following arrest in November 1987 of leader Osamu Maruoka indicate that JRA may be organizing cells in Asian cities, such as Manila and Singapore. Has had close and longstanding relations with Palestinian terrorist groups—based and operating outside Japan—since its inception.

Activities: During the 1970s, JRA conducted a series of attacks around the world, including the massacre in 1972 at Lod Airport in Israel, two Japanese airliner hijackings, and an attempted takeover of the U.S. Embassy in Kuala Lumpur. In April 1988, JRA operative Yu Kikumura was arrested with explosives on the New Jersey Turnpike, apparently planning an attack to coincide with the bombing of a USO club in Naples and a suspected JRA operation that killed five, including a U.S. servicewoman. Kikumura was convicted of these charges and is serving a lengthy prison sentence in the United States. In March 1995, Ekita Yukiko, a longtime JRA activist, was arrested in Romania and subsequently deported to Japan. Eight others have been arrested since 1996, but leader Shigenobu remains at large.

Strength: About eight hard-core members; undetermined number of sympathizers.

Location/Area of Operation: Location unknown, but possibly based in Syrian-controlled areas of Lebanon.

External Aid: Unknown.

al-Jihad a.k.a. Egyptian al-Jihad, New Jihad, Egyptian Islamic Jihad, Jihad Group

Description: Egyptian Islamic extremist group active since the late 1970s. Appears to be divided into two factions: one led by Ayman al-Zawahiri—who currently is in Afghanistan and is a key leader in terrorist financier Osama bin Ladin's new World Islamic Front—and the Vanguards of Conquest (Talaa' al-Fateh) led by Ahmad Husayn Agiza. Abbud al-Zumar, leader of the original Jihad, is imprisoned in Egypt and recently joined the group's jailed spiritual leader, Shaykh Umar Abd al-Rahman, in a call for a "peaceful front." Primary goal is to overthrow the Egyptian government and replace it with an Islamic state. Increasingly willing to target U.S. interests in Egypt.

Activities: Specializes in armed attacks against high-level Egyptian government officials. The original Jihad was responsible for the assassination in 1981 of Egyptian President Anwar Sadat. Appears to concentrate on high-level, high-profile Egyptian government officials, including cabinet ministers. Claimed responsibility for the attempted assassinations of Interior Minister Hassan al-Alfi in August 1993 and Prime Minister Atef Sedky in November 1993. Has not conducted an attack inside Egypt since 1993 and never has targeted foreign tourists there. Has threatened to retaliate against the United States, however, for its incarceration of Shaykh Umar Abd al-Rahman and, more recently, for the arrests of its members in Albania, Azerbaijan, and the United Kingdom.

Strength: Not known, but probably several thousand hard-core members and another several thousand sympathizers among the various factions.

Location/Area of Operation: Operates in the Cairo area. Has a network outside Egypt, including Afghanistan, Pakistan, the United Kingdom, and Sudan.

External Aid: Not known. The Egyptian government claims that Iran, Sudan, and militant Islamic groups in Afghanistan—including Osama bin Ladin—support the Jihad factions. Also may obtain some funding through various Islamic nongovernmental organizations.

Kach a.k.a. the Repression of Traitors, Dikuy Bogdim, DOV, the State of Judea, the Committee for the Safety of the Roads, the Sword of David, Judea Police, Forefront of the Idea, The Qomemiyut Movement, The Yeshiva of the Jewish Idea and Kahane

Chai a.k.a. Kahane Lives, the Kfar Tapuah Fund, The Judean Voice, The Judean Legion, The Way of the Torah, The Yeshiva of the Jewish Idea, KOACH

Description: Stated goal is to restore the biblical state of Israel. Kach (founded by radical Israeli-American rabbi Meir Kahane) and its offshoot Kahane Chai, which means "Kahane Lives," (founded by Meir Kahane's son Binyamin following his father's assassination in the United States) were declared to be terrorist organizations in March 1994 by the Israeli Cabinet under the 1948 Terrorism Law. This followed the groups' statements in support of Dr. Baruch Goldstein's attack in February 1994 on the al-Ibrahimi Mosque—Goldstein was affiliated with Kach—and their verbal attacks on the Israeli government.

Activities: Organize protests against the Israeli government. Harass and threaten Palestinians in Hebron and the West Bank. Have threatened to attack Arabs, Palestinians, and Israeli government officials. Claimed responsibility for several shootings of West Bank Palestinians that killed four persons and wounded two in 1993.

Strength: Unknown.

Location/Area of Operation: Israel and West Bank settlements, particularly Qiryat Arba' in Hebron.

External Aid: Receives support from sympathizers in the United States and Europe.

Kurdistan Workers' Party (PKK) a.k.a. Partiya Karkeran Kurdistan

Description: Established in 1974 as a Marxist-Leninist insurgent group primarily composed of Turkish Kurds. In recent years has moved beyond rural-based insurgent activities to include urban terrorism. Seeks to establish an independent Kurdish state in southeastern Turkey, where the population is predominantly Kurdish.

Activities: Primary targets are Turkish government security forces in Turkey but also has been active in Western Europe against Turkish targets. Conducted attacks on Turkish diplomatic and commercial facilities in dozens of West European cities in 1993 and again in spring 1995. In an attempt to damage Turkey's tourist industry, the PKK has bombed tourist sites and hotels and kidnapped foreign tourists.

Strength: Approximately 10,000 to 15,000. Has thousands of sympathizers in Turkey and Europe.

Location/Area of Operation: Operates in Turkey, Europe, the Middle East, and Asia.

External Aid: Has received safe haven and modest aid from Syria, Iraq, and Iran. The Syrian government claims to have expelled the PKK from its territory in October 1998.

Liberation Tigers of Tamil Eelam (LTTE) a.k.a. Tamil Tigers, Ellalan Force. Known front organizations: World Tamil Association (WTA), World Tamil Movement (WTM), the Federation of Associations of Canadian Tamils (FACT), the Sangillan Force

Description: The most powerful Tamil group in Sri Lanka, founded in 1976. Uses overt and illegal methods to raise funds, acquire weapons, and publicize its cause of establishing an independent Tamil state. Began its armed conflict with the Sri Lankan government in 1983 and relies on a guerrilla strategy that includes the use of terrorist tactics.

Activities: Has integrated a battlefield insurgent strategy with a terrorist program that targets not only key government personnel in the countryside but also senior Sri Lankan political and military leaders in Colombo. LTTE political assassinations and bombings have become commonplace, including suicide attacks against Sri Lankan President Ranasinghe Premadasa in 1993 and Indian Prime Minister Rajiv Gandhi in 1991. Has refrained from targeting Western tourists out of fear that foreign governments would crack down on Tamil expatriates involved in fund-raising activities abroad. Prefers to attack vulnerable government facilities and withdraw before reinforcements arrive.

Strength: Approximately ten thousand armed combatants in Sri Lanka; about three thousand to six thousand form a trained cadre of fighters. The LTTE also has a significant overseas support structure for fund-raising, weapons procurement, and propaganda activities.

Location/Area of Operation: Controls most of the northern and eastern coastal areas of Sri Lanka and has conducted operations throughout the island. Headquartered in the Jaffna Peninsula, LTTE leader Velupillai Prabhakaran has established an extensive network of checkpoints and informants to keep track of any outsiders who enter the group's area of control.

External Aid: The LTTE's overt organizations support Tamil separatism by lobbying foreign governments and the United Nations. Also uses its international contacts to procure weapons, communications, and bomb-making equipment. Exploits large Tamil communities in North America, Europe, and Asia to obtain funds and supplies for its fighters in Sri Lanka. Some Tamil communities in Europe also are involved in narcotics smuggling.

Mujahedin-e Khalq Organization (MEK or MKO) a.k.a. Mujahedin-e Khalq, the National Liberation Army of Iran (NLA, the militant wing of the MEK), People's Mujahedin Organization of Iran (PMOI), National Council of Resistance (NCR), Organization of the People's Holy Warriors of Iran, Sazeman-e Mujahedin-e Khalq-e Iran, Muslim Iranian Student's Society (front organization used to garner financial support)

Description: Formed in the 1960s by the college-educated children of Iranian merchants, the MEK sought to counter what it perceived as excessive Western influence in the Shah's regime. Following a philosophy that mixes Marxism and Islam, has developed into the largest and most active armed Iranian dissident group. Its history is studded with anti-Western activity, and, most recently, attacks on the interests of the clerical regime in Iran and abroad.

Activities: Worldwide campaign against the Iranian government stresses propaganda and occasionally uses terrorist violence. During the 1970s the MEK staged terrorist attacks inside Iran and killed several U.S. military personnel and civilians working on defense projects in Tehran. Supported the takeover in 1979 of the U.S. Embassy in Tehran. In April 1992 conducted attacks on Iranian embassies in thirteen different countries, demonstrating the group's ability to mount large-scale operations overseas.

Recent attacks in Iran include three explosions in Tehran in June 1998 that killed three persons and the assassination of Asadollah Lajevardi, the former director of the Evin Prison.

Strength: Several thousand fighters based in Iraq with an extensive overseas support structure. Most of the fighters are organized in the MEK's National Liberation Army (NLA).

Location/Area of Operation: In the 1980s the MEK's leaders were forced by Iranian security forces to flee to France. Most resettled in Iraq by 1987. In the mid-1980s did not mount terrorist operations in Iran at a level similar to its activities in the 1970s. In recent years has claimed credit for a number of operations in Iran.

External Aid: Beyond support from Iraq, the MEK uses front organizations to solicit contributions from expatriate Iranian communities.

National Liberation Army (ELN) a.k.a. the Ejercito de Liberacion Nacional

Description: Pro-Cuban, anti-U.S. guerrilla group formed in January 1965. Primarily rural based, although has several urban fronts, particularly in the Magdalena Medio region. Entered peace talks with Colombian Civil Society in mid-1998 and was preparing to participate in a national convention in early 1999.

Activities: Conducted weekly assaults on oil infrastructure (typically pipeline bombings) and has inflicted massive oil spills. Extortion and bombings against U.S. and other foreign businesses, especially the petroleum industry. Annually conducts several hundred kidnappings for profit, including foreign employees of large corporations. Forces coca and opium poppy cultivators to pay protection money and attacks government efforts to eradicate these crops.

Strength: Approximately three thousand to five thousand armed combatants and an unknown number of active supporters.

Location/Area of Operation: Colombia, border regions of Venezuela.

External Aid: None.

Palestine Islamic Jihad-Shaqaqi Faction a.k.a. PIJ-Shaqaqi Faction, PIJ-Shallah Faction, Palestinian Islamic Jihad (PIJ), Islamic Jihad of Palestine, Islamic Jihad in Palestine, Abu Ghunaym Squad of the Hizballah Bayt Al-Maqdis

Description: Originated among militant Palestinians in the Gaza Strip during the 1970s; a series of loosely affiliated factions rather than a cohesive group. Committed to the creation of an Islamic Palestinian state and the destruction of Israel through holy war. Because of its strong support for Israel, the United States has been identified as an enemy of the PIJ. Also opposes moderate Arab governments that it believes have been tainted by Western secularism.

Activities: Has threatened to retaliate against Israel and the United States for the murder of PIJ leader Fathi Shaqaqi in Malta in October 1995. Conducted suicide bombings against Israeli targets in the West Bank, Gaza Strip, and Israel. Has threatened to attack U.S. interests in Jordan.

Strength: Unknown.

Location/Area of Operation: Primarily Israel and the occupied territories and other parts of the Middle East, including Jordan and Lebanon. The largest faction is based in Syria.

External Aid: Receives financial assistance from Iran and limited assistance from Syria.

Palestine Liberation Front–Abu Abbas Faction a.k.a. the Palestine Liberation Front (PLF), PLF–Abu Abbas

Description: Broke away from the PFLP-GC in mid-1970s. Later split again into pro-PLO, pro-Syrian, and pro-Libyan factions. Pro-PLO faction led by Muhammad Abbas (Abu Abbas), who became member of PLO Executive Committee in 1984 but left it in 1991.

Activities: The Abu Abbas-led faction has conducted attacks against Israel. Abbas's group also was responsible for the attack in 1985 on the cruise ship *Achille Lauro* and the murder of U.S. citizen Leon Klinghoffer. A warrant for Abu Abbas's arrest is outstanding in Italy.

Strength: At least fifty.

Location/Area of Operation: PLO faction based in Tunisia until *Achille Lauro* attack. Now based in Iraq.

External Aid: Receives support mainly from Iraq. Has received support from Libya in the past.

Popular Front for the Liberation of Palestine (PFLP) a.k.a. the Red Eagles, the Red Eagle Group, the Red Eagle Gang, the Halhul Gang, the Halhul Squad

Description: Marxist-Leninist group founded in 1967 by George Habash as a member of the PLO. Joined the Alliance of Palestinian Forces (APF) to oppose the Declaration of Principles signed in 1993 and has suspended participation in the PLO. Broke away from the APF, along with the DFLP, in 1996 over ideological differences. Has made limited moves toward merging with the DFLP since the mid-1990s.

Activities: Committed numerous international terrorist attacks during the 1970s. Since 1978 has conducted numerous attacks against Israeli or moderate Arab targets, including killing a settler and her son in December 1996.

Strength: Some eight hundred.

Location/Area of Operation: Syria, Lebanon, Israel, and the occupied territories.

External Aid: Receives most of its financial and military assistance from Syria and Libya.

Popular Front for the Liberation of Palestine–General Command (PFLP-GC)

Description: Split from the PFLP in 1968, claiming it wanted to focus more on fighting and less on politics. Violently opposed to Arafat's PLO. Led by Ahmad Jabril, a former captain in the Syrian Army. Closely tied to both Syria and Iran.

Activities: Has conducted numerous cross-border terrorist attacks into Israel using unusual means, such as hot-air balloons and motorized hang gliders.

Strength: Several hundred.

Location/Area of Operation: Headquartered in Damascus with bases in Lebanon and cells in Europe.

External Aid: Receives logistic and military support from Syria and financial support from Iran.

al-Qa'ida a.k.a. al Qaeda, "the Base," the Islamic Army, the World Islamic Front for Jihad Against Jews and Crusaders, the Islamic Army for the Liberation of the Holy Places, the Osama bin Laden Network, the Osama bin Laden Organization, Islamic Salvation Foundation, The Group for the Preservation of the Holy Sites

Description: Established by Osama bin Ladin about 1990 to bring together Arabs who fought in Afghanistan against the Soviet invasion. Helped finance, recruit, transport, and train Sunni Islamic extremists for the Afghan resistance. Current goal is to "reestablish the Muslim State" throughout the world. Works with allied Islamic extremist groups to overthrow regimes it deems "non-Islamic" and remove Westerners from Muslim countries. Issued statement under banner of "The World Islamic Front for Jihad Against the Jews and Crusaders" in February 1998, saying it was the duty of all Muslims to kill U.S. citizens, civilian or military, and their allies everywhere.

Activities: Conducted the bombings of the U.S. embassies in Nairobi, Kenya, and Dar es Salaam, Tanzania, on August 7, 1998 that killed at least 301 persons and injured more than 5,000 others. Claims to have shot down U.S. helicopters and killed U.S. servicemen in Somalia in 1993 and to have conducted three bombings targeted against the U.S. troop presence in Aden, Yemen, in December 1992. Linked to plans for attempted terrorist operations, including the assassination of the pope during his visit to Manila in late 1994; simultaneous bombings of the U.S. and Israeli embassies in Manila and other Asian capitals in late 1994; the midair bombing of a dozen U.S. trans-Pacific flights in 1995; and a plan to kill President Clinton during a visit to the Philippines in early 1995. Continues to train, finance, and provide logistic support to terrorist groups that support these goals.

Strength: May have from several hundred to several thousand members. Also serves as the core of a loose umbrella organization that includes many Sunni Islamic extremist groups, including factions of the Egyptian Islamic Jihad, the Gama'at al-Islamiyya, and the Harakat ul-Mujahidin.

Location/Area of Operation: The embassy bombings in Nairobi and Dar es Salaam underscore al-Qa'ida's global reach. Bin Ladin and his key lieutenants reside in Afghanistan, and the group maintains terrorist training camps there.

External Aid: Bin Ladin, son of a billionaire Saudi family, is said to have inherited around $300 million that he uses to finance the group. Al-Qa'ida also maintains money-making businesses, collects donations from like-minded supporters, and illicitly siphons funds from donations to Muslim charitable organizations.

Revolutionary Armed Forces of Colombia (FARC) a.k.a. Fuerzas Armadas Revolucionarias de Colombia

Description: The largest, best-trained, and best-equipped insurgent organization in Colombia. Established in 1964 as a rural-based, pro-Soviet guerrilla army. Organized along military lines and includes several urban fronts. Has been anti-United States since its inception. The FARC agreed in 1998 to enter into preliminary peace talks with the Colombian government. The Pastrana administration demilitarized five large rural municipalities to meet FARC conditions for peace talks. (President Andres Pastrana traveled to this area on January 7, 1999 to inaugurate peace talks with guerrilla leaders, although the FARC's most senior leader failed to attend.)

Activities: Armed attacks against Colombian political, economic, military, and police targets. Many members pursue criminal activities, carrying out hundreds of kidnappings for profit annually. Foreign citizens often are targets of FARC kidnappings. Group has well-documented ties to narcotics traffickers, principally through the provision of armed protection for coca and poppy cultivation and narcotics production facilities, as well as through attacks on government narcotics eradication efforts. Also began a bombing campaign against oil pipelines in 1998.

Strength: Approximately eight to twelve thousand armed combatants and an unknown number of supporters, mostly in rural areas.

Location/Area of Operation: Colombia, with occasional operations in border areas of Venezuela, Panama, Peru, Brazil, and Ecuador.

External Aid: None.

Revolutionary Organization 17 November (17 November) a.k.a. Epanastatiki Organosi 17 Noemvri

Description: Radical leftist group established in 1975 and named for the student uprising in Greece in November 1973 that protested the military regime. Anti-Greek establishment, anti-U.S., anti-Turkey, anti-NATO, and committed to the ouster of U.S. bases, removal of Turkish military presence from Cyprus, and severing of Greece's ties to NATO and the European Union (EU). Possibly affiliated with other Greek terrorist groups.

Activities: Initial attacks were assassinations of senior U.S. officials and Greek public figures. Added bombings in 1980s. Since 1990 has expanded targets to include EU facilities and foreign firms investing in Greece and has added improvised rocket attacks to its methods.

Strength: Unknown, but presumed to be small.

Location/Area of Operation: Athens, Greece.

External Aid: Unknown.

Revolutionary People's Liberation Party/Front a.k.a. Devrimci Sol (Revolutionary Left), Dev Sol, Devrimci Halk Kurtulus Partisi-Cephesi (DHKP/C), Dev Sol Silahli Devrimci Birlikleri, Dev Sol SDB, Dev Sol Armed Revolutionary Units

Description: Originally formed in 1978 as Devrimci Sol, or Dev Sol, a splinter faction of the Turkish People's Liberation Party/Front. Renamed in 1994 after factional infighting, it espouses a Marxist ideology and is virulently anti-U.S. and anti-NATO. Finances its activities chiefly through armed robberies and extortion.

Activities: Since the late 1980s has concentrated attacks against current and retired Turkish security and military officials. Began a new campaign against foreign interests in 1990. Assassinated two U.S. military contractors and wounded a U.S. Air Force officer to protest the Gulf War. Launched rockets at U.S. consulate in Istanbul in 1992. Assassinated prominent Turkish businessman in early 1996, its first significant terrorist act as DHKP/C.

Strength: Unknown.

Location/Area of Operation: Conducts attacks in Turkey—primarily in Istanbul—Ankara, Izmir, and Adana. Raises funds in Western Europe.

External Aid: Unknown.

Revolutionary People's Struggle (ELA) a.k.a. Epanastatikos Laikos Agonas, Revolutionary Popular Struggle, Popular Revolutionary Struggle, June 78, Organization of Revolutionary Internationalist Solidarity, Revolutionary Nuclei, Revolutionary Cells, Liberation Struggle

Description: Extreme leftist group that developed from opposition to the military junta that ruled Greece from 1967 to 1974. Formed in 1971, ELA is a self-described revolutionary, anti-capitalist, and anti-imperialist group that has declared its opposition to "imperialist domination, exploitation, and oppression." Strongly anti-U.S. and seeks the removal of U.S. military forces from Greece.

Activities: Since 1974 has conducted bombings against Greek government and economic targets as well as U.S. military and business facilities. In 1986 stepped up attacks on Greek government and commercial interests. Raid on a safehouse in 1990 revealed a weapons cache and direct contacts with other Greek terrorist groups, including 1 May and Revolutionary Solidarity. In 1991, ELA and 1 May claimed joint responsibility for more than twenty bombings. Greek police believe they have established a link between the ELA and the Revolutionary Organization 17 November.

Strength: Unknown.

Location/Area of Operation: Greece.

External Aid: No known foreign sponsors.

Shining Path (Sendero Luminoso, SL) a.k.a. Partido Comunista del Peru en el Sendero Luminoso de Jose Carlos Mariategui (Communist Party of Peru on the Shining Path of Jose Carlos Mariategui), Partido Comunista del Peru (Communist Party of Peru), PCP, Socorro Popular del Peru (People's Aid of Peru), SPP, Ejercito Guerrillero Popular (People's Guerrilla Army), EGP, Ejercito Popular de Liberacion (People's Liberation Army), EPL

Description: Larger of Peru's two insurgencies, SL is among the world's most ruthless guerrilla organizations. Formed in the late 1960s by then university professor Abimael Guzman. Stated goal is to destroy existing Peruvian institutions and replace them with peasant revolutionary regime. Also wants to rid Peru of foreign influences. Guzman's capture in September 1992 was a major blow, as were arrests of other SL leaders in 1995, defections, and Peruvian President Alberto Fujimori's amnesty program for repentant terrorists.

Activities: Has engaged in particularly brutal forms of terrorism, including the indiscriminate use of bombs. Conducted fewer attacks in 1998, generally limited to rural areas. Almost every institution in Peru has been a target of SL violence. Has bombed diplomatic missions of several countries in Peru, including the U.S. Embassy. Conducts bombing campaigns and selective assassinations. Has attacked U.S. businesses since its inception. Involved in cocaine trade.

Strength: Approximately two thousand armed militants; larger number of supporters, mostly in rural areas.

Location/Area of Operation: Rural based, with few violent attacks in the capital.

External Aid: None.

Tupac Amaru Revolutionary Movement (MRTA) a.k.a. Movimiento Revolucionario Tupac Amaru

Description: Traditional Marxist-Leninist revolutionary movement formed in 1983. Aims to rid Peru of imperialism and establish Marxist regime. Has suffered from defections and government counterterrorist successes in addition to infighting and loss of leftist support.

Activities: Bombings, kidnappings, ambushes, assassinations. Previously responsible for large number of anti-U.S. attacks; recent activity has dropped off dramatically. Most members have been jailed. Nonetheless, in December 1996, fourteen MRTA members overtook the Japanese ambassador's residence in Lima during a diplomatic reception, capturing hundreds. Government forces stormed the residence in April 1997, rescuing all but one of the remaining hostages. Has not conducted a significant terrorist operation since.

Strength: Believed to have fewer than one hundred remaining members.

Location/Area of Operation: Peru.

External Aid: None.

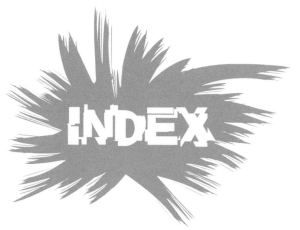